T0117094

God's Best Gift,
In an ugly Wrapping

Onyemaechi Emmanuel Okoro

authorHOUSE®

AuthorHouse™
1663 Liberty Drive
Bloomington, IN 47403
www.authorhouse.com
Phone: 1-800-839-8640

Published by AuthorHouse 6/4/2013

ISBN: 978-1-4817-6028-7 (sc)
ISBN: 978-1-4817-6026-3 (hc)
ISBN: 978-1-4817-6027-0 (e)

Library of Congress Control Number: 2013910095

Any people depicted in stock imagery provided by Thinkstock are models,
and such images are being used for illustrative purposes only.
Certain stock imagery © Thinkstock.

This book is printed on acid-free paper.

Because of the dynamic nature of the Internet, any web
addresses or links contained in this book may have changed
since publication and may no longer be valid.

The views expressed in this work are solely those of the author
and do not necessarily reflect the views of the publisher, and
the publisher hereby disclaims any responsibility for them.

Acknowledgement

I am using this opportunity to thank my beloved wife, Rose - Akwaugo, whose inexhaustible love and support has brought a lot of joy to our family, and to my precious children: Ezinne, Chiamaka and Onyemaechi II, for their support and prayers while getting this book ready.

My special gratitude to my elder brother, Hon. Eberechukwu - Boniface whose support and guidance brought out the best in me, and my sister Chinyere - Agatha for her prayers.

Where do I start to thank my cousin, Dr Mathew N. Ibewiro, who is my best friend and my great fan. I don't know what I would do without you.

I am deeply indebted to my friend and mentor, Prof. James Strazzella whose immeasurable kindness and support can never be forgotten. God will continue to bless you abundantly.

I cannot thank you enough, Prof. Gerald J. A. Nwankwo, a gifted man, whose encouragement and guidance helped me to complete this book. What can I tell you, my buddy, Prof. Dr. Chieke Evans Ihejirika, a venerated educator, I know I can always count on you; your invaluable suggestions and corrections are highly appreciated.

I also thank my friends Dr. James Nwachukwu, Vita Oguledo, Anthony Njoku - Õsuji, Ricky Moors, Chief Johny Amugo, Paschal Osuji, and Dr. Emmanuel Nmagu - Ede-Nimo, for their consistent support to me. And, my dear friend Dr. Ugo Anusionwu, the Action man, whose unflinching support is inestimably treasured.

I am very thankful to all of you, who have supported me in many ways, especially Chi Achi, Dr. (Judge) Anthony Rulli and Judge Rui and Marina Cascaldi, and other friends I could not list due to space and time.

I cannot close without thanking Fr. Kieran Udeze - ome-ihe-ukwu of Iwena Tansi Igbo Community Chaplaincy, Philadelphia, Pennsylvania, USA, whose support and prayers have been inspirational to me. God bless you.

All errors in this book are completely mine.

DEDICATION

This book is dedicated to my parents of the blessed memories: Ignatius and Maria, and my brother Linus and sister, Angelina, who are also serving the Lord in heaven.

QUOTE

"Never let the fear of fall becloud your ambition, we all fall at one point in life or another. Your zeal to rise should not go down with you. Raise your hand each time you fall, for your rescue may be closer than you know."

Author

FOREWORD

O. Emma. Okoro's *God's Best Gift* is an epiphany. It is an epiphany because Okoro reveals the image of God to his readers through his personal experiences. *God's Best Gift* gives several accounts of the presence of God among His people, a God from whom all things come, a God by whom every endeavor is consummated, and a God in whom everything is made perfect. It is this art of revelation that makes Okoro's *God's Best Gift* a family companion. In a distinctive storytelling voice, Okoro invites his readers to follow him through what Mark Twain describes as "everyman's" journey, a journey through the dark alley when hope seems hopeless, yet for people with faith and hope, it culminates in a spiritual communion with God, when God takes over from where humanity stops.

Okoro manifests that God always watches over His own, and that is why He is always willing and ready to intervene whenever He seeks out one of His because to Him, every creation has the a special worth, including the perfect and the not-so-perfect, including Saint Paul, including Saint Augustine. In his own simple way, as he journeys to the phone booth in South America,

Okoro doesn't know what is going to happen next, but God watches over His own. In *God's Best Gift*, Okoro demonstrates that when God wants His own, He goes for them; it is God who seeks out His own.

Okoro encourages his readers to know God and go to Him through prayers. He believes that prayers will help believers stand out conspicuously where God will seek them out because He is watching.

The conversational voice of *God's Best Gift*, its simplicity of language, and the possibility of its theme make me proud to recommend it to any family that has a roof to share with God; it is an invaluable travel ticket to a celestial banquet.

----------- Gerald J. A. Nwankwo ------------

© April, 2013

DOES GOD EXIST?

//

The question whether or not God exists is not a simple question. It has a lot of intricacies both in definition and understanding. There are various people who have difficulties believing in the existence of God due to philosophical, theological or logical reasons, and there are many others who wonder why any person, basically, would doubt anything about God. The explanation of "who God is", and his creation of the world, is ungraspable within an ordinary human representation, mostly with the concept that God has no Beginning and created the earth from nothing. We can only assimilate it as most other mysteries embodied in our faith.

Within or outside all the constructive and comparative theories and hypothesis, Aristotle's notion was: "Since God, as ultimate final cause, is the perfection toward which all things tend and since thinking is the most perfect activity with which we are familiar, the best analogue for God's nature is thinking."[1]

We would like to, but would not have the opportunities, to discourse the generality of God. Let's particularize this idea by firstly, reflecting on this God's real entity. The thinking and reasoning about God Being is one of "the highest forms that man's knowledge of God can take: 'to know that we do not know God insofar as we recognize that God's essence lies beyond all that which we know of him.'"[2] As Pope John Paul II dissected in one of his teachings: "Since our knowledge of God is limited, our language about him is equally so. We can name God only by taking creature as our starting point, and in accordance with our limited human ways of knowing and thinking."[3] And, Aquinas did not relent in his notion that irrespective of our impression of God which might change, as man always does, but this does not signify a change in the Creator, but only a change in us.[4]

To further this deliberation here, it will be condensed to the 'existence of God', most especially, attempting to enhance our understandings based on [our] faith and common knowledge. Considering from both the ancient and contemporary scholars, and from the paradigm of their arguments and inquisitions, it becomes imperative to be allied with Thomas Aquinas, the Doctor of the Church, who after elaborate synthesis of the Platonic, Aristolelian and other philosophical scholars of virtue and theological thinkers, in conjunction with those who patently integrated the existential realization, has affirmed that there is God. "God is that Being Whole whose nature it is to exist. ... God is existence in itself."[5]

Through the vagaries of thought and understanding, and without prejudice to a more careful intellectual and spiritual examination, Augustine said "there is God. To God, all that transpires is intelligible and reasonable. God is omniscient, but also omnipotent. All that is, is of God; creation is encompassed by God and dwarfed by him. Appearances are only complicated shadows cast by simple realities we will never fully comprehend."[6]

Malebranche, a great scholar of talent, through his doctrine of occasionalism, try to advance it when he explained: "God's will is the cause of anything's existing at any particular time and place. Since God's will is all-powerful, it is impossible that any created power could move something against God's will. Hence, nothing is moved except by God."[7] The rational is that everything is God, or manifestation of God.[8]

REVEALING GOD

///

The quest for the invisible nature of God, and the mysterious creation of the earth from nothing than by His mere words: "let there be light and there was light," which was a display of splendor, coupled with the plurality of his person, mostly when He said: "Let us make man in our image, after our likeness," (Gen. 1: 26). Having put a human face on the invisible Being, this stirred implosive curiosity and marathon of discovery from some scholars about him.

The creation of Adam and his corporeal appearance, gave the first glimpse of God's physiology to look like a man but, it became big issues to unravel who the "Us" and "Our" are and how they originated. Though it was the first divine revelation of His nature before the birth of Jesus which happened many centuries thereafter; consequentially, mirrored God as having head, hands, legs, eyes and body like the human. This exposition mangled the human inquisition of Him instead of explaining who He really was.

Immediately after the complete creation of the earth, God did not hesitate to make Himself available to Adam but could not be seen. In the evening, Adam and Eve heard the voice of the Lord God walking in the Garden. (Gen. 3: 8). They recognized the voice because they had been familiar with it.

God beautified the Garden of Eden, blessed everything in it before providing it to Adam. Though Adam was put in dominion of all the creatures, he was also directed on God's expectation of him in the Garden. Adam never saw God's physical being but he had a good relationship with Him and maintained appropriate communication channel. Adam loved the Garden and everything in it. That was the best moment of his life.

God's manifestations to people thereafter by means of talking to them and appearing in the invisible manners are not enough to quench the curiosity of those who wanted to see him fully and acknowledge His real physique. He had good interactions with Jacob like He did with Abraham, (Genesis 17:1) and after blessing Jacob and renaming him Israel, He declared: "I am almighty God!"[11] (Genesis 35: 11). "I will walk among you, and will be your God, and you shall be my people." (Leviticus 26: 12). He told the Israelites long after, to look upon Him until the end of the earth for "I am God, and there is none else." (Isaiah 45: 22).

God continued to prove Himself when He told the Israelites that he is the same God who brought all of them out of the land of Egypt to save them from being slaves and to give them back their dignity (Leviticus 26:13). "I was with you in the wilderness and in the great drought" (Hosea 13: 5). God never lacked in making his voices heard by his people.

The earth population continued to increase and multiply reaching to the time of Moses who asked to see God's glory.

God identified the rock he wanted Moses to stand on and Moses was notified: "And when my glory passes by, I will put you in the cleft of [this] rock and cover you with my hand until I passed. Then I will remove my hand and you shall see my back, but not my face." (Exodus 33: 21 - 23).

The children of Israel continued having difficulties comprehending who this their God was, the God who had promised them the land flowing with milk and honey, but continued to hide Himself. "What is his name?" - they asked Moses, if we cannot see him at least, trying to know what Moses called Him.

Although God was disappointed on how feeble minded and insatiable the Israelites were about him, but He made more effort to explain himself. God did not want to complicate his relationship with the Israelites by exposing himself excessively to them. He asked Moses to tell them again: "I am Who I am" and, that He was the God of their fathers - Abraham, Isaac and Jacob" (Exodus 3:14 -16).

When Moses tried to explain things to the Israelites, they did not believe him, they did not listen to him; worse still, they made him to look like a liar who was making up stories that he was seeing God (Exodus 4:1).

KNOWING GOOD AND EVIL

W hy has man been so inquisitive about God: trying to know His origin, His end and all about His existence?

The answer is not far away. Remember that the devil was a disobedient angel who was chased out of heaven. He knew what was good and evil because his eyes were already opened beyond human ability. Adam himself only knew the good and had no idea what evil could be because the garden of Eden was new with everything in it as provided by God. Adam was the one that named the animals and birds in the garden. There was no comparison since there was no other like it.

The glory of the garden was not half enjoyed when God cut it short. When Eve, the wife of Adam was responding to the serpent who came to confuse and induce her to disobey God, she notified the serpent that God wanted them to enjoy every fruit in the garden except the fruits at the center tree which they should not eat because they would die if eaten. (Genesis 3: 3).

The serpent laughed over it, because he knew that Eve was a novice who didn't know much. Again, he knew that Eve didn't know what death meant because she had never experienced any. The only companion Eve had in the garden was her husband Adam and had not seen anything dead. By all indications, they were not created to die. The deceptive character of the devil is simple but the result is obvious.

"You shall not die," the serpent told Eve - whatever it meant to her, but "you would be like God, seeing good and evil" (Genesis 3: 5). Though Eve did not know what evil was but she visualized that God had created wonderful things in the garden and she could find herself doing the same things God did. Telling her that she would know good and evil could sound to her like colors - seeing red and purple, all of them are beautiful and could be the things found in the garden. But the information that fascinated her was the opportunity to acquire the power to be like God. This should be the origin of greed and envy on earth. She began to consider herself competing with God if she could acquire the same power as God had.

Like she didn't want to waste time about it, she grabbed one of the forbidden but good looking fruits and ate. She did not die immediately, making the serpent momentarily credible that she would not die. When one was a kid, if you were told for the first time never to touch fire because it would burn you, when that instruction is disobeyed, and you put your hands in the fire, you would see an instant result - burn. It was not the result here.

There was no knowledge of Eve's immediate reaction when she did not die after eating the fruit against the order of God. She must have been curiously expecting some changes or surprises in herself as the serpent promised her that she would begin to know between the good and the evil. She was still in confusion.

From all indications, nothing strange happened to Eve from the time she ate the apple until her husband came home. As if the apple tasted good too, she quickly took one and gave to her husband. It is not clear if the apple given to Adam had been plucked earlier or Eve plucked it when Adam came home. Whichever way, Adam ate it without any hesitation.

God wanted to know how Adam behaved, being the man he put in-charge of all his creatures, the person who should have known better than any other. Although the serpent did not go to Adam in person neither did they have any discussion at any time, but God was disappointed with him and He took instant action. The behavior of Adam should not be characterized as an accident because the forbidden fruit was special and very different from all others. To Eve in particular, the fruit was pleasant (Genesis 3: 6). It's difference from other fruits were clear. There shouldn't have been any confusions.

It was obvious that Adam loved his wife Eve so much, and probably could not have resisted what Eve gave to him. Could it be the origin of the saying that "love is blind, making him incapable of seeing or thinking?" The effect was devastating. It was like mixing up the medications your doctor told you that can not go together. Disobeying the serious instructions from God showed an unimaginable catastrophic consequence.

"Adam! Where are you?" God called. "I am naked" (Genesis 3: 10). From then they began to realize the difference between the good and evil. Eve now understood the saying from the serpent that she would know between the good and evil, then she realized that she had been fooled . Greed.

Because God had declared to Adam that he would die any time he ate the fruit, God revoked the blessing given to the land, and allowed them to experience the consequence of their disobedience: "All your life you sweat to master the ground, until your dying day. Then you will return to the ground from which you come. For you were made from the ground and to the ground you will return" (Genesis 3: 17 - 19). Eventually, Adam and his wife - Eve came to know for the first time what death was all about, returning to the ground. "When Adam sinned, sin entered the entire human race. His sin spread death throughout all the world, so everything began to grow old and die, for all sinned" (Romans 5:12).

Adam and Eve were on their own, facing the consequences of their actions. Irrespective of the calamity the devil had caused them, it did not give the devil enough satisfaction. It was only two victims down and he was waiting for more. That weapon which had worked for the devil against man - "you will be like God," he has not given it up.

The devil had been in heaven and knew how beautiful the heaven is. The devil was not happy that it lost its glory in heaven because of its disobedience to God. It is like stealing money from your boss and when caught and fired, you could not start your own business nor could you get another job. Definitely, you would not be a happy person. And, the devil would not want to go this journey alone; that's the reason it went to work early on Eve to get more subordinates.

Unlike what He did to Adam, God did not condemn the disobedient angel (devil) to death when sent down from heaven. Being a former angel of God, it was more powerful than man and God knew that. Man can't come close to the monstrous power of the devil. "Sin has pulled mankind so low that no right to divine favor remains. The favor that comes is free and unearned, a gift from above."[9] But God has thrown a life jacket to man - prayer and secondly, sending his son, Jesus on a rescue mission.

BIRTH OF JESUS

The coming of Jesus at the contemporary time gave the world a better opportunity to know how God looks. His physique was almost like that of Adam. Jesus caught deep into people's curiosity when he began to proclaim and clarify that He and His Father are one, and any person that has seen him has seen his father who is in heaven (John 10: 30).

It sounded satisfactory, and probably should have put an end to the doubts about God - the Father's physical being, having seen His replica coupled with the combination and fulfillment of all the related prophecies which had been debated ages before. It did not. The tendency which could have closed the physiological and resemblance argument, instead generated more questions than answers. Philip, one of the followers of Jesus still asked him: "Lord, show us the Father and we will be satisfied" (John 14: 8). This request did not indicate the people had accepted the answer to this same problem of physical God, regardless of all the teaching and explanations from Jesus about Himself and His Father.

The most troubling point is when the question was coming from someone who had been following Jesus and had been a witness to some of the miracles He had been performing. But, Philip seemed to be speaking for others too as he asked: "show us" (and not show me). After rebuking him, Jesus reassured all again: "I am in the Father and the Father is in me" (John 14:10).

The true knowing of God and worshiping him with grace has always been a challenge to man. God has always been free and available to man but, either by ignorance, darkened understanding or blindness of the heart (Ephesians 4:18) the access and comprehension of Him seem burdened and complicated.

Jesus understood the confusion his disciples were having about his person when he put them to test. "Who do people think that I am?" he asked them. Some of them replied that he was called John the Baptist, some said Elias, Jeremias and others said one of the prophets. He threw the question back to them by asking: "Whom do you think I am?"

They started looking at each other. None of them knew the answer except Peter who responded: "The Christ, the Messiah, the Son of the living God;" others marveled how Peter knew the answer. Jesus quickly intervened and commented that it was an answer revealed to him by His Father, He blessed Peter and made him the head of his disciples (Matthew 16:13 -19).

The acquirable knowledge from this experience is that it needs commitments to know God and understand his value. It may not be something a person can do alone unless by having the connection with God. It is only God alone who can reveal, provide and direct our thoughts to Himself. You may not achieve this alone as the other disciples could not. You need to connect yourself to God as you need to connect your television to power to make it work. It is called prayer and it is the only means and instrument to get power and light from the Creator.

Fighting the Devil

A man of God is like a soldier in the battle field, always ready to fight, and must be well equipped by his General with all the available and necessary modern weaponry, including the night vision gurgle, rocket launcher and bunker buster, as to fight the enemy to the end. The way the weaponry are used would however depend on the soldier. If he throws away everything and tries to capture the enemy with his bare hand, he would face the resultant consequence. Being with God and fighting for His cause, we look through the people who by describing and explaining the nature of their works manifest this quality. "We glorify the soldier as the [person] absolutely unincumbered. Owning nothing but his bare life, and willing to toss that up at any moment when the cause commands him [or her] ..."[10] Mr. Voysey explained better: "That nearness of God is a constant security against terror and anxiety. It is not that they are at all assured of physical safety, or deem themselves protected by love which is denied to others, but that they are in a state of mind equally ready to be safe or to meet with injury. If injury befall them, they will be content to bear it because the Lord is their keeper, and nothing can befall them without His will. If it be His will, then injury is for them a blessing and no calamity at all."[11] When you turn off the feelings of fears and anxieties, and let go the importance you attach to cosmetic life, making a willing self surrender for various Godly reasons, you will perceive the love and tranquility of Christ in your heart.

Miracles do happen but since the fight between David and Goliath, no one has witnessed such an easy and colossal victory ever again. The fight against the devil needs a good preparation with strong and modern weaponry. You cannot take the devil for granted. Peter told his faithful to be sober and vigilant so that their adversary will not devour them (1 Peter 5:8).

The devil has put into the subconscious mind of man that he as man can be like God. It has not been erased. From the time of Adam to date, the actions of man point negatively toward that direction - being like God. Man has only one goal in life, to discover the physical God, decode his secrets and compete with him. In defining the behavior of man, Pope John Paul II said: "The beginning of this spiritual battle goes back to the moment when man "abused his liberty at the urging of personified Evil and set himself against God and sought to find fulfillment apart from God.'"[12]

Man has gone beyond verifications, for better for worse, searching for God and the secrets to his inventions and innovations. They have gone to the moon and all the planets, under the sea, and also attempting to reach to the sun in search of God. The smartest thing God has done is keeping the secret of Himself to Himself.

The Author's Personal Prayer

My dear Lord, God
I entrust unto thee my body and soul.
Hear the voice of my supplication
And look upon me with thy mercy.
I do not have the integrity
To come unto thee, Oh Lord!

Make me to walk your paths;
You are my rock and my fortress.
You have known my soul in adversities;
Forgive, bless and give me peace;
You are the forgiving God
That asked me to boast in thee.

Do not dwell on my weaknesses;
My flesh and my heart faileth
Deliver me from all my iniquities
And give me the power and energy
To be victorious by your special grace;
Let your glory be above the earth.

You have been my shelter
And the tower of my pride.
What would I do without you, Lord?
Where would I go without your salvation?
What would I do if you were not my refuge?
You made me harmonious in thee.

You have chosen me from the crowd,
Be not far from me.
I will go in thy strength,
Increase thy holiness in me.
My lips will praise and sing unto thee
Until I rest with thee forever.

****

Thank you Lord, Jesus Christ
For shedding your precious blood
To cleanse my condemned sin
You said: "it is finished"
And I have a complete new life.

Let not the evils of the world
Stand between you and me.
Shine your light on me always
For my adversaries to know
That I am your protected child.

When you hear my cry, Lord
When the sea is stormy,
And my boat is rocked,
Manifest to the world the wonders
That come from the infallible God.

Let your work be my testimony
Show the world that you never changed,
Guide and protect your loved one.
At the end of my lease on earth, Oh Lord
May I glorify you in your Kingdom. Amen.

****

Holy Mary, Mother of our savior, Jesus Christ
Queen of the Immaculate hearts,
The most humble and merciful lady
Who by special grace bore the only son of God,
And through Him the world received salvation.

The matron of the poor and the powerless,
I fall into thy caring arms
Knowing that you will never fail me;
Take my pleas to your beloved son
Who can never turn you down.

The most faithful and devoted mother,
By the special merit of your son, Jesus
And your humble supplication on my behalf,
My fears will turn to victory
And my cries to laughter.

Remember, Oh most merciful Mother
That I am weary and worrisome;
My loads are heavy and the journey long,
I run unto thee for protection
Through your loving son, Jesus Christ.

Your intercessions on my behalf
Before your son are never left unanswered
Oh worthy mother of all ages,
May your loving kindness and compassion
Secure for me everlasting favor from your son, Jesus Christ.

CONNECTION WITH GOD

rayer is the communication network between us and God. Sometimes, whether right or wrong, I compare it to an insurance coverage - you get coverage against the unforeseeable danger. You put yourself, health, journey, business, profession, education, families and everything that is important to you in life to the protection of God. All the things that are within and beyond of your control are covered. Prayer can be a conveyer belt that takes in and out your luggage and consignments to God. But to the faithful, it is also your armor against the devil: "we express awareness of our relationship with God. We are creatures who are not our own beginning, not the master of adversity, not our own last end..."[13]

A French theologian was clarifying the connection with God during the time of prayer; he genuinely explained that it is "a conscious and voluntary relation, entered into by a soul in distress with the mysterious power upon which it feels itself to depend, and upon which its fate is contingent."[14] While distinguishing this intermingling transaction with God, the writer postulated that prayer is an act of religion, and "[r]eligion is nothing if it be not the vital act by which the entire mind seeks to save itself by clinging to the principle from which it draws its life."[15]

If you cannot pray due to the weakness of the body or mind, while chasing fame, wealth or a mere comfort, you expose yourself and your life to the risk of destruction. You are at the mercy of the devil and the devil doesn't know any mercy. Prayer is the blood line of the sick, the companion of the lonely, protector of the suppressed, light of the blind, comforter of the widow, defender of the poor, water for the thirsty, food for the hungry and everything for the world. It is undisputable that prayer builds your immunity against temptation and evil.

When Herold the King was persecuting the disciples of Jesus, he killed James with his sword and his citizens applauded him. He apprehended Peter, imprisoned him under the guard of sixteen soldiers with intent to kill him after the Passover. They maximized their security against Peter by chaining him between two soldiers, and the others were standing to deter his escape.

The King had no rivalry, especially at the time he was famous with his actions against the Christians. The Church declared a war of prayers against King Herold; praying incessantly for Peter's protection and release (Acts 12: 1 - 5).

Time was running out and Peter was about to be executed on the following day; "suddenly there was a light in the cell and an angel of the Lord stood beside Peter, smote him on the side, and raised him up" (Acts, 12 : 6- 7).

The chains and shackles on Peter's hands and legs fell off. Peter who seemed to be in a trance, was instructed by the angel to dress up. Peter was taken through the tight prison security to the outside gate, and the angel asked him to go. It was there that Peter realized where he was and what God had done for him. He thanked God for his rescue (Acts, 7 - 11).

The Holy Angel serves God with honor.

God's miraculous manifestation is not only in the bible; Gerald was a soldier who was fighting to protect his people against the genocidal atrocities from their adversaries. His number one weapon was his prayer - his daily supplication to God for safety and his rosary for the intercession of Mary, the Mother of God. His second weapon was his gun.

One day, he was fighting at one of the fiercest and bloodiest battle fields of that war history, and Gerald was captured by the enemies. As a patriotic and vibrant young officer who refused to yield one inch of his fatherland to the enemies, it made him popular at that war sector, and having inflicted a lot of injuries and destructions on his enemies, to say he was tortured when captured was an understatement.

"I ... prayed so hard and intently" Gerald confessed, "[and] the angels and saints in heaven were looking out for me..."[16] The captors handed him over to the commanding officer who was notoriously brutal and cruel. According to the commander's record, he shot most of his captives without any regards. Worse, Gerald having been an officer that inflicted a lot of casualties at them, it was expected from the commander to dehumanize him before determining what to do to him, expectedly getting him killed.

Like Daniel in the lion's den, the sadist commanding officer was sympathetic to Gerald than punishing him more. The enemy officer who others saw as a terror was received by the commander like a gallant soldier, and was asked how he acquired his boldness to fight them. The captors who brought him to the commander opened their mouths in dismay. Gerald who had said his last Hail Mary could not believe how his life was spared.

Though he was taken as a prisoner of war, it was hard to explain how he walked away from death. He regained his freedom at a later time and never stopped praising God:

The Lord is my shepherd;

I shall not want.

He maketh me to lie down in green pastures:

He leadeth me beside the still waters.

He restoreth my soul:

He leadeth me in the path of righteousness

for his name sake

Yes, though I walk through the

dark valley of death,

I will fear no evil:

For thou art with me;

Thy rod and thy staff they comfort me.

Thou preparest a table before me

In the presence of mine enemies:

Thou anointest my head with oil;

My cup runneth over.

Surely goodness and mercy

Shall follow me all the days of my life:

And I will dwell

in the house of the Lord for ever. (Psalm 23)

You do not wait for things to happen before you talk to your God. He is always there for you, ready and able to respond to your request. God is like electricity, you have to be connected to get energy. "Prayer is an opportunity to let in what would otherwise be left out. Air is there if we breathe, light is there if we open our eyes."[17] "You need to develop your own relationship with God, for God relates to you as an individual. Developing a personal relationship with God allows you to tap into [His] promises...."[18] It is essentially individualistic when interacting and unveiling yourself and your past negativity to God, and having been blind to prayer until you met God's unfailing presence which transformed from indulgence to mercy. Prayer can be an organizing force in you to achieve what you could not realize in any other manner. "We and God have business with each other; and in opening ourselves to his influence our deepest destiny is fulfilled."[19]

It is important to know that you would be fantasying your destiny if you begin your relationship with God based only on what you want from Him, and not for the interest of serving Him. No matter the path you want to take in your relationship with God, it has to be original and authentic. "You can not borrow that relationship, you must possess it for yourself."[20] Acknowledge to God that he is your Father and also show that you are his obedient child.

One of the most important things you should give deep consideration when meditating, is to be ready to embrace God. Seek you will find; knock and the door will be opened to you (Matt. 7:7). When you are knocking on God's door with your prayers, you have to listen attentively because God may be talking to you without your hearing him. A lot of times people have questioned the ability God gave them to solve problems, and they talked themselves to defeat. There have been several people who complained that God didn't answer their prayers, but couldn't understand that they were actually answered.

Again, God may be knocking on your door without your knowing it. When God called Samuel for the first time, Samuel did not recognize His voice nor did he expect that God could call him for a special message. It was Eli who educated him on how to identify God's voice. Having been informed and given the knowledge on how God could call, Samuel was more prepared to hear from Him. When Samuel was called again, he responded effectively: "Speak, for your servant is listening" (1 Samuel 3: 10). What about you? Are you listening to the Lord? Can you recognize his voice? Do you need more prayers to recognize God's presence?

Remember the saying of the Lord: "Behold, I stand at the door, and knock: if anyone hears me and opens the door, I will come in and enjoy fellowship with him and he with me" (Rev. 3 :20). "To hear God in this life we must truly want to hear Him and be ready to accept the message that comes from Him. The message will come from deep inside, telling us what is right and what is wrong with our lives."[21]

Augustine's life is a motivating and inspiring example why you must continue to search for God's profound understanding and unseasonable grace and compassion. It is never late to effect a positive change in your life by putting God in the driver's seat. It doesn't matter when God calls you, every one in heaven is rewarded equally.

Remember the parable of the laborers, referring to the Kingdom of Heaven; a man invited laborers to work in his vine yard. He was hiring the new laborers at the intervals. Though he bargained with each laborer separately, he offered all of them equal wages irrespective of their hours of work. He hired laborers from morning until evening. Some worked longer hours while others worked limited hours, but at the end of the day, the man paid every one what he agreed with them. The laborers who worked longer hours grumbled about the equal pay. And, the man replied: "Didn't you agree to work at the rate you were paid? Should you be angry because I am kind?" (Matthew 20: 1 - 15).

The exigency, or the harmonious perspective was to encourage a voluntary reversion to God without any penal consequences. No matter the time you return to God, you will not lose your benefits in heaven. Consider the kind gesture Jesus showed to the thief who repented at the last minute on the cross when crucified with Him, the thief begged Jesus not to forget him in His kingdom; Jesus said unto him: "Today, you will be with me in Paradise. This is a solemn promise" (Luke 23: 42 - 43). Another indispensable feature was about the prodigal son who collected his inheritance from his wealthy father and squandered them at a distant country. When he realized his iniquity, he repented and returned to his father and apologized. He said to his father: "I have sinned against heaven and against you; I [do not deserve] to be called your son" (Luke 15 : 21). His father was gratified on his son's repentance and return to his house. He designated his servants to organize an elaborate festivity because his son who "was dead ...has come to life again; he was lost, and has been found" (Luke 15: 24).

We cannot forget about David; when prophet Nathan was sent by God to inform David about his condemnation because of his children's unabated transgression, David prayed to God: "Don't keep looking at my sins - erase them from your sight. Create in me a new, clean heart, O God fill me with clean thoughts and right desires" (Psalms 51: 9 - 10).

There are people who established selfish purposes by making something else more central and significant to their happiness than their relationship to God, and they went through blind alleys before finding their way to God. When you have a healing in your heart, and take away obstacles in your paths so as to stimulate your mind, you will experience a new passion and a higher level of wisdom. Augustine's early life was burden of inadequacies, confusion, prodigality, controversies and preoccupations, both in habit and actions. Like Saul called Paul, no one expected he would be redeemed through a divine mystery.

During this period which Augustine lived through contumacious and assortment of delusional world, his mother Monica, was heavily disturbed. She prayed fervently, asking God for only a favor: to touch her son's life with His magisterial power. Her unbending and unbroken demand from God yielded a mystic result. Augustine was converted, and became an unprecedented asset of the church.

When Monica realized God had performed the miracle that transformed and illuminated her son's life, she felt fulfilled and said: "My God hath done this for me abundantly, that I should now see thee withal, despising earthly happiness, become his servant: what am I doing still here?"[22]

Augustine could not fully understand what happened to him, but he was fired-up by the love and wisdom of his new found life. He said to God:

31

Too late I loved Thee,
O Thou Beauty of ancient days, yet ever new!
too late I loved Thee!
And behold, Thou wert within, and I abroad,
and there I search for Thee;
Deformed I, plunging amid those fair forms,
Which Thou hast made.
Thou wert with me, but I was not with Thee.
Things held me far from Thee,
which, unless they were in Thee, were not at all.
Thou called, and shouted, and burst my deafness.
Thou flashed, shone, and scattered my blindness.
Thou breathed odors, and I drew in breath
and I sigh for Thee.
I tasted, and hunger and thirst
Thou touched me, and I burned for Thy peace.[23]

Augustine manifested unrivalled and distinguished
sophistication of thoughts and expression in spreading the gospel.
He asked God not to excavate his past but to clear the stage for
him to move forward. He unreservedly offered himself to God:

Let me know Thee, O Lord, who knowest me:
Let me know Thee, as I am known.
Power of my soul,
enter into it, and fit it for Thee,
That Thou mayest have and hold it
Without spot or wrinkle.
This is my hope, therefore do I speak.[24]

It was in consonance with the thought and experience of Stephen H. Bradley when he said: "I had an ardent desire that all mankind might feel as I did; I wanted to have them all love God supremely. Previous to his time I was very selfish and self-righteous; but now I desired the welfare of all mankind, and could with a feeling heart forgive my worst enemies, and I felt as if I should be willing to bear the scoffs and sneers of any person, and suffer anything for His sake, if I could be the means in the hands of God, of the conversion of one soul."[25]

You have two other important reasons to pray, one, to thank God for the good things being done for us without your asking for them, both the ones you know and the unknown, even good things you don't truly deserve because of your behaviors. You run away from God when you think everything is fine with you and think only having your merriments. You ignore Him when you have enough for yourself, or seem not to need any further support for any reasons. When you are fascinated with your well-being or consumed in the admiration of the earthly things, you forget God. Upon all that, He gives you life and makes Himself available to you.

The second reason to pray is to maintain the link - the Spiritual unity with God; to communicate and interact with Him at all times. It is "... indeed the source of strength for sustaining what is wavering. Then it is that there is born a confidence like the confidence expressed by St. Paul in his words: 'There is nothing that I cannot master with the help of the One who gives me strength.' "[26] "It is important that intimate conversation with the heavenly Father never be absent from [y]our daily existence."[27]

It gives a shower of tears reading about the revelation and conversion of David Rose in prison. "After many years of running from God, I reached the point of being totally empty and without any hope. It was an opening to grace. Instead of despairing and turning bitter, as I had done many times in the past, I cried in anguish over the person I had become. God showed me the pain I had caused to those I claimed to love the most. He showed me that I had crucified the innocent love of Christ"[28]

St. Thomas Aquinas expressed that the word of God abiding in us should be continually in our thoughts, since not only should we believe in Him, but also meditate upon Him; otherwise we would derive no profit from His presence. "In fact, meditation of this kind is of great assistance against sin"[29] Fr. James Martin helped us to understand the challenges that affect our momentum to attain such a task when he explained: "Many of us lead busy lives and are constantly rushing around. As a result, it's hard to slow down and, as the saying goes, 'smell the roses.' That can be a problem because it means we often don't pause to take stock of life's blessings. Moreover, we seemed to be hardwired to pay closer attention to problems rather than to blessings"[30]

Some of your problems are self made, and you blame God later about them. You build rocky roads, causing you to stumble and fall, or overloading your feelings with the vanity of mortal things which fail to satisfy you even when you get them. Since life is only what you deem it to be, you can only find happiness and satisfaction in yourself. You have set yourself goals and hopes based on your selfishness and shortsightedness; things you try to accomplish without the spiritual power or grace.

Even when you try to navigate through your life by stepping out of yourself, Solomon said: "And I gave my heart to seek and search out by wisdom concerning all things that are done under heaven: this sore travail hath God given to the sons of man to be exercised therewith. I have seen all the works that are done under the sun; and, behold all is vanity and vexation of spirit" (Ecclesiastes 1: 13 - 14).

We have heard a lot of times that looks can mislead; we also know the old adage which said that not all that glitter are gold. Let me take a few examples from the flowers we use in decorating our houses and offices; some of them are not our best friends as they smell wonderfully with beautiful foliages. The monkshood plant has one of the most beautiful flowers - with mix of blue, white and/or pink colors. However, if the fluid from this adoring plant is ingested by accident, it will cause numbness of the tongue, blurred vision and irregular heart rate; Nerium oleander which is one of the gorgeous plants people want around their homes, has one of the deadliest leaves because they are extremely poisonous. What seems to be beautiful may have a hidden dark side.

There is a cause for everything that happens to us whether for good or bad. Interestingly, God knows it all. It is through prayer that we ask for the things we rightly desire and the ones we simply get from His kindness. We learn that "prayer not only teaches us to ask, but also directs all our affections."[31] God has given us the opportunity to survive countless challenges, why shouldn't we be optimistic to survive many more? "Trusting that our lives are divinely guided gives us the courage to surrender our will and have faith that all is happening as it should"[32]

This is one of the most beautiful prayers Pope John Paul II shared with us:

Holy Father, friend of all creatures,
everlasting in your Word
you loved us and thought of us
and wished us to recognize your face
In the face of your Only Begotten
Born of Mary.
In him, tested in everything like us,
Except sin,
You suffered our weaknesses;
In him your mercy extends
From generation to generation forever.
Holy Father,
See your people
As, after celebrating the memory
Of the Passion and death of the Lord,
They follow the Way of the Cross,
Praying in expectation of the Resurrection.
We share your Son's cry of pain,
Its echo continuing in the cry
That goes up from the countless crosses
Of men and women of all epochs.
We are in communion
With his offering of love,
While his Passion draws to a close:
In the tragic period

Of suffering and death
We pray that the trusting dialogue of us children
With you, Father
In the Spirit of your Son
May never cease.
He lives and reigns forever and ever.[33]

THE MOST IMPORTANT PRAYERS

///

Despite all other ways and means to make your petition to God, my analogy is that there are two cardinal and indispensable ways to pray. The Lord's prayer as was taught by our Lord Jesus and the Hail Mary by her Church, have shown to be the most humble intercession of the mother of Jesus. Both Jesus and his mother Mary are the Father and Mother of all prayers.

Let me start with the Lord's Prayer. It is a petition to God that envelops anything you are as a human being, including but not limited to your state of mind, your acknowledgement of his sovereignty over you, humility to him, sincerity in your relationship with him, your motive for the request you are making from God and your disposition to obey him and worship Him always. Augustine defined this prayer as the medium of spirituality.

It is hard to believe but true that some disciples of Christ who had spent a lot of time with him, seeing all the miracles and revelation from him could not articulate their prayers in effective manners. Either they were confused and could not prepare themselves adequately or they did not know what to ask from God, having been with Jesus, his son for so long. To pray properly means a complete submissive and articulate devotion, reflection and supplication to God.

When Hamilton was having his challenges of life, fighting the odds that were lacerating and wrenching his existence, he encountered difficulties gathering his pieces together. As the obstacles seemed to be insurmountable, his mind dwindled. Though he grew up around religious relations but he didn't know what to do with his faith.

He ran to God and prayed: " I've been trying to do this for so long and I can't do it anymore. I can't try anymore, because I've failed on my own. So if you would help me do this, I'll do whatever. You do with me what you want to do with me. But I surrender"[34]

God looked at the sincerity of his surrender and accepted Hamilton's petition and sent a rescue brigade of angels to him. His life was turned around and so many positive things began to happen to him. He was appreciative to God and never wanted to fall into that deep hole of despair which almost consumed his life.

When the disciples of God found themselves in such swampy situations, it was only one of them who was courageous enough to go to Jesus for enlightenment. He requested: "Lord, teach us to pray" (Luke 11: 1). Having noticed their weaknesses, and ignorance, Jesus did not hesitate to direct them on how to pray.

He instructed that any one who wants to pray, should pray like this:

Our Father which art in Heaven,
Hallowed be they name,
Thy kingdom come.
Thy Will be done on earth, as in heaven.
Give us this day our daily bread
And forgive us our trespasses,
as we forgive those who trespass against us.
And lead us not into temptation;
but deliver us from evil (Luke 11:2-4).

Looking at this short prayer, it sounds simple and easy but it is not. We will breakdown the prayer as we try to assimilate it. The whole prayer gives us the guidance on how to direct our thoughts and mind, and to make a pious expression of our concern and to demand the expectative answers from God. But taking a deep thought and having a pause, you will see a lot of challenges and commitments on you before you continue with your requests from God and the expectant results. You need to roll away rocks and debris on the high way to reach your destination. Unfortunately, the weight and size of this debris are personalized by God.

First, Jesus directs you that it is humility to recognize your Father's Power over you, to glorify his name before making a total surrender of yourself and your problems. Jesus knows how merciful His Father has been to the angels, saints and other residents in Heaven, and He wants you to ask for the same favors on earth. You should put God in-charge of yourself and in all that you do.

Jesus warned us about greed; that is one of the desires the serpent used against Eve. You can never feel fulfilled when you have avaricious appetite. Do not be selfish by asking for yourself more than is necessary. God may be asking: "Why do you ask for one week or one month food when you don't even know if you will last that long? Why asking for many years of material things when you don't know how many days left for you? Why are you worried for the good things being done for others when I gave you more than you need? Why are you not satisfied with the things given to you when some of your good friends have not received anything? Just ask for your daily needs and your Father who loves you will take it from there." You cannot starve. God will feed you like He feeds the birds and the animals in the forest and those of them at the dry deserts. Even the ants are not starving. The most important of all is to know how to ask.

You want God to be kind, sympathetic and merciful to you. He puts the same responsibility on you to show these same favors to other people too. Don't go to God asking for a favor when you cannot do the same for your brother, sister, neighbor and other people around you. "Forgive our sins as we forgive those who sinned against us." he commanded us. We get burdened when we are stuck in our old feelings and would not let go the bad feelings we have for others. We understand the obligations of God to be caring and forgiving but, when hardhearted or overzealous, we do not realize how God is hurt by our disobedience, disaffection, greediness, envy and cruelty to others.

The disputes and quarrels against each other will not give us access or a gateway to embrace God's passionate love reserved for us in his infinite happy home, being heaven. You cannot love the invisible God without loving the visible human beings living with you here on earth. He wants you to be in peace with yourselves on earth. "Blessed are the merciful: for they shall obtain mercy" (Matthew 5: 7). "But I say to you: Love your enemies! Pray for those who prosecute you! In that way you will be acting as true sons of your Father in heaven. He gives sunlight to both the evil and the good, and sends rain on the just and the unjust too" (Matthew 5: 44 - 45).

Jesus in all his teachings never minced words on what he wants us to be and what we can ask from his Father in heaven. He was very transparent when declaring that the most important of all his commandments is to love God with all your heart, soul, mind and strength, and to love your neighbor as you love yourself. It is more important than any other sacrifices you can make to God (Mark 12: 29 - 31). Any backdoor to reach God will be unrealistic.

It is hard to forgive your enemy; to pray for someone who never cared for you, who killed your mother, father or other loved ones; someone who destroyed your business and future, or someone who betrayed your trust in him or her and inflicted you with unbearable pains and putting you on crushing emotional state: but that's exactly the people God wants you to forgive. "Since you have been chosen by God who has given you this new

43

kind of life, and because of his deep love and concern for you, you should practice tenderhearted mercy and kindness to others. Be gentle and ready to forgive; never hold grudges. Remember, the Lord forgave you, so you must forgive others" (Colossians 3: 12 - 13). Some great thinkers said that "It is merely the extreme limit of a kind of magnanimity with which, in the shape of pitying tolerance of our oppressors, we are fairly familiar. Yet if radically followed, it would involve such a breach with our instinctive springs of action as a whole, and with the present world's arrangements, that a critical point would practically be passed, and we should be born into another kingdom of being."[35]

You may have a million other justifiable reasons not to forgive any of your enemies; there have been people who became blind, lame or bed-ridden because of other people's hateful actions. And God wants you to forgive this people? There are certain moments you will say to yourself that it is really hard to cultivate this forgiving heart when you could easily revenge but, it is this hard feelings that God has given you the order to relinquish; commanding and tasking that this forgiveness must be done, basing it on His own concept of love and not yours. Yes, a message from the God that gave you life, unconditional hope and family.

On a second thought, you don't really need to forgive your enemy, it's a matter of choice. It becomes mandatory to listen and obey if you intend to seek any favor from God, no matter how little. If you have a perfect life and, are in control of your life and destiny, you don't need to ask God for anything though He has voluntarily been providing you with those things you pride yourself with. Right? The problem is this, is there any individual with a perfect life? Is there any individual in control of his tomorrow? The conditions in the Lord's prayer are only for those who want God's intervention in their lives. God knows life is a puzzle and there will be no individual who will not need His support to put this puzzle together. Most importantly, where do you go after life without God?

Even though God protects our affairs and wants us to depend on his providence with joy-filled spirituality, He does not force his love, faith or himself on us. "He reveals himself to us as free human beings, and our faith response to him is made within the context of our freedom"[36] It is important to understand unequivocally that Jesus is the only Lord who, if you receive him, will fulfil you completely, and if you fail him, will forgive you eternally.[37] If you deny God, you are worshipping fantasy which will fail you.

THE FORGIVING HEART

God does not want to make life unnecessarily rough for us, but he doesn't want us to be like the wicked servant who owed his master over ten thousand talents and could not afford to pay back. When his master wanted to sell him and all the members of his family; he fell on the ground begging for patience and tolerance until when he could be able to pay.

The servant's master was filled with compassion and mercy, and he forgave him all his debt and told him to go. The servant was happy and left. It did not take long, the servant saw a fellow servant who was owing him few talents and he took the fellow servant by the throat, asking him to pay all that he owed him. The fellow servant fell to the ground begging him to have patience until he could pay. He refused to have any patience but went ahead in casting his fellow servant in prison until he could pay all his debt (Matthew 18: 23 - 30).

That's exactly the blank check God is avoiding to give you. If you cannot forgive your neighbor as God has forgiven you, your neighbor may be swallowed up with overmuch sorrow (2 Corinthians 2: 7). "Do to others what you want me to do for you," God demands. Jesus lived exemplary life so that you can have love without boundaries; that's what He wants you to bestow on others. Remember when Jesus was betrayed and was about to be arrested, one of His disciples who wanted to defend his Master, took his sword and struck off one of the ears of the high priests' servants; Jesus picked up the ear, put it back and healed the servant. Jesus knew He could defend Himself if He wanted to fight back. Even his father could send him battalions of angels if push came to shove but it was not his choice. He turned back to his disciple and cautioned him on the use of force: "Put back your sword to its sheath, He that goes by the sword dies by the sword" (Matthew 26: 51 - 52; Luke 22: 50 - 51).

If you are fighting evil, you cannot behave like an evil person. Remember the story of the animals trying to unify to fight against man's cruelty to them; they believed that man had been killing them for various reasons and they wanted to come together to fight back. While the gathering was going on, the cat spotted the rat and wanted to take advantage of the gathering to catch the rat; Major, who was the leader of the animals and was using his position to solicit for comradeship so that all the animals would fight with one spirit and speak with one voice against man, noticed the behavior of the cat, he was disappointed and he called on all the animals: "I merely repeat, remember always your duty of enmity towards Man and all his ways ... And remember also that in fighting against Man, you must not come to resemble him."[38]

Jesus preached on many aspects about forgiveness and also showed an ultimate and defining example at the end of his sojourn

48

on earth; after the extreme physical anguish and mental torture, he found a place in his heart to forgive all the people involved: "Father, forgive them; for they don't know what they are doing" (Luke 23: 34).

The conclusion of the Lord's prayer: "Lead us not into temptation but deliver us from all evil" seem to be the most challenging part of the prayer. Jesus knows that this world is a sloppy, snaky, scorpion infested, den of lions and wolves terrain. You can be victimized by your own actions or by other people's actions. The prayer is like asking God: "Please don't allow the devil to use others against me and don't allow me to be used by the devil against others." Tough nuts!

The work of the devil could happen in many shapes and dimensions. Temptations! We all know the story of Job and I don't know how many people today who can go half way what Job did. We could have been living in the garden of Eden today if not the temptation of Adam and Eve. The same devil is still alive with his agents, tireless and hovering all over the places seeking for an opportunity to strike again and again.

There was a story of a married pastor who was dating a wife of his church member. Pathetically, the church member trusted his pastor and was telling him all his family secrets including random quarrels with his wife. It was through this interaction that the pastor found out that his church member had a life insurance of almost one million dollars. The pastor connived with the man's wife (his mistress) and they killed the innocent man in order to get his money.

It was like a professional job how the man was killed because nobody knew the culprits of this heinous crime. The autopsy showed that he died of gun shot wounds. Both the pastor and the unsuspected widow attended the man's funeral ceremony and the pastor even prayed for him. The man's wife, now widow, collected the insurance money and split it with her coconspirator - the pastor. They succeeded in their plot to assassinate an innocent man but, to survive maintaining the secret of the crime was another challenge. The devil that told them that they could do it left them immediately it completed its mission. They were left alone to battle with their consciences and consequences of their actions.

As days went by, the woman's conscience began to trouble her. It got worse day by day until when she could not control herself any more. The money she collected did not matter much to her and she started regretting all her actions. She felt so guilty and became depressed. As she began to think on how she would free herself from this self inflicted bondage, she prayed her ex-husband for forgiveness. There is no clear evidence that a dead person can forgive; but the prayer didn't seem to be helping her life, while her emotional conditions were spinning out of control. She reported herself to the police and confessed her crime.

She and the pastor were arrested and charged for the murder. With her cooperation with the police, she was given less than ten years in jail and the pastor got life. The wife of the pastor and her children who were not involved, were baffled at what the devil could do.

"Deliver us from all evil." One could be victimized for no just cause but just by being at the wrong place at the wrong time. There could be many other terrible stories of what the devil can do; another story was about a family man, working hard to sustain his family but was shot dead while returning home after a long day at work. The criminal who killed him was arrested and when asked by the police what his motives were, he said he was drunk, and on drugs and felt like killing somebody on the street. The innocent man lost his life, impromptu and for nothing. You can imagine why you should not pass any day without reciting this Lord's prayer.

How fast do we expect response from God when we pray? There is no doubt that we want instant results, if possible, happening as we ask for them. God knows that too. Unfortunately, it does not go that way, at least, most of the times. Why?

You get your results as fast as your requests are processed in heaven. Remember the prayer asking God's will be done on earth as it is in heaven. Another practical understanding is that God cannot be hurried. He has infinite attention to the complains and prayers of all eternity in a split of a second. "We are saved by Hope" and that means looking forward to getting what we are asking from God. "But if we must keep trusting God for something that hasn't happened yet, it teaches us to wait patiently and confidently" (Romans 8: 24 - 25).

The Lord's prayer is a complete revealed embodiment of your life and ways on earth. Your life here, sometimes beautiful, jolly and hilarious, and at other times, rough, cruel, depressing and inhospitable. There are all kinds of temptation and evil challenges coming your ways. Jesus didn't mean to scare you but to put you on guard and to beckon for God's intervention and protection at all times.

The second Prayer: **The Hail Mary**

Hail Mary
Full of Grace
The Lord is with Thee
Blessed art thou amongst women
And Blessed is the fruit of thy womb - Jesus!
Holy Mary mother of God
Pray for us sinners now
And at the hour of our death.
Amen.

MOTHER OF MERCY

T he most fascinating part of this prayer, to me, is the second segment - asking the Mother of God to pray for us "now and at the hour of our death." We are people in panic who believe that anything could happen to us at any moment of our lives; that's why we need the intercession at every period of our day and at all places; to secure her motherly watchful eyes on us and most especially, when we are parting finally from this earth. The hour of death is the most compelling moment of our lives: "the separation and release of the soul from our body."[39] We ask her to intercede for us, the merciful Mother of Jesus whose request is never ignored.

We all are conversant with the story of Mary before the conception of Jesus, being a humble and compassionate lady who was chosen by God to bring His only Son to earth in form of a man. God chose her because He knew she was the right woman that could handle the big task associated with the coming of Jesus. God needed a woman with strong resilience both in flesh and spirit.

When the angel, the messenger of God came to Mary, he said to her: "... you are full of grace and have found favor with God. He has chosen you and you are blessed as the best among women." Mary did not comprehend the message. She never heard anything like that before either to herself or to any other woman. Again, considering her humble background, she never expected to be put in such a dignified position.

Observing that Mary had been frightened, the angel quickly strengthened her, and assured that the Lord was with her. "The Holy Ghost shall come upon thee, the power of the Highest shall overshadow you" (Luke 1: 28 - 35). It was telling her that she would never be herself again as the power from above would take total control of her. "In a wholly singular way she cooperated by her obedience, faith, and burning charity in the Savior's work of restoring supernatural life to souls. For this reason she is a mother to [all men and women] in the order of grace."[40] We fly to her patronage because she will always be there for the faithful, "a sign of certain hope and comfort to the pilgrim People of God."[41] "Mary's function as mother of men in no way obscures or diminishes this unique mediation of Christ ..."[42]

Mary did not manifest if she had enough understanding of the responsibility bestowed onto her by God, but she acknowledged the immense privilege that God found such favor in her. She did not arrogate herself with the visitation of the angel, but accepted the message with her natural humility as she responded: "Behold the handmaid of the Lord; be it unto me according to thy word" (Luke 1: 38). From then the challenge and responsibility as a mother emanated and she became, and continued to be the mother of Jesus and to the world. She never fell short of any expectations from God and her blessings were not in short supply.

From the birth of Jesus, Mary took her responsibility seriously as she raised her son. She continued to be prayerful and obedient to God, particularly as she started to notice unparallel intelligence and wonders about her son - Jesus who, by the special design of God, began to grow in strength and enormous manifestation of knowledge and wisdom. At the age of twelve, he escaped the watchful guard of his parents and went to the temple where he was teaching doctors and elders. All of them that heard him were astonished at his understanding of the scripture and answer to their questions (St. Luke 2:45 - 47).

Jesus has a special relationship with His mother. His obedience to his mother has been undoubtedly permanent. Mary never second guessed if her son would obey her requests at any time. Though she did not know her son's calendar, she had the intuition of a mother.

During the marriage ceremony in the village of Cana in Galilee (John 2:1 - 7), Mary was there with her son Jesus and His disciples. The ceremony seemed to be going well until Mary was told that the hosts had run out of wine supply. Jesus who had never performed any open miracles was there. Going into the substantive discussion, the revelation would be that the hosts were related to Mary for her to be at the ceremony with her son, and to be notified when the wine was finished. Again, this must have been an issue of shame and embarrassment to run short of wine supply during a wedding ceremony by the Jewish culture. With this in mind, Mary, knowing the potential of her son, went to him, and asked him to do something to abate the humiliation.

"... My hour is not yet come." Jesus responded to his mother. But Mary was confident that her son would not disappoint her at that distressful moment. She instructed the servants: "Do whatever He tells you to do" (John 2: 1).

It did not take long after his mother talked to him, Jesus performed his first miracle when he told the servants to fill six water pots with water. When that was done, he transformed the water to wine and it was the best wine at the event.

This is a typical relationship between Jesus and His mother Mary. She is a compassionate mother and her lovely and infinite bond continued from Jesus' childhood to his death. Remember the time of Harold, when the king was trying to kill Jesus; at God's instruction, Joseph was told to run away with Jesus and his mother to the land of Egypt to save the child's life (Matt.2: 13). It was the first trauma for Mary, hearing that her son was about to be killed. At the end of Jesus sojourn on earth, during his crucifixion, his mother was there for him too. When most of his friends, relatives and disciples had escaped, Jesus looked down from the cross and saw his mother standing by him (John. 19: 25 - 26). That is why you should always occupy your "whole [life] with one thought and one desire of love, that [you] may love not for the sake of merit, not for the sake of perfection, not for the sake of virtue, not for the sake of sanctity but for the love."[43]

With such an inseparable affection, who would have such a mother and turn down her request? Even I, as an ordinary person, would not look away from the request of my own mother, whom I loved dearly; I wouldn't want to be anywhere without her. I know my mother (of the blessed memory) is now in heaven looking over me and all her children, interceding for us in conjunction with the holy mother of God to secure our salvation. My mother showed me an unqualified love from my childhood till the time she went to heaven.

When we ask for our Holy Mother's intercession with all our hearts and in good faith, we know she will listen and convey our messages to her son. Her motherly attention is very important in our daily lives mostly, during the times we are helplessly in danger of our health, finance, children, parents and loved ones. Most importantly, we need her during our final transition, when we are on our destination to the world no human has gone and came back to earth. We are always asking her to plead on our behalf for clemency so that God will request for our souls only for his own nobler purpose.

The time of death is the fulfillment of the condemnation of God: "For you were made from the ground, and to the ground you will return" (Genesis 3:19). The body is only the clay that God molded and breathed life into it, and when that air of life escapes, it leaves the body in its original form - the clay. At death, the body is like a deflated balloon.

HUMAN BLACK BOX

When a plane crashes and the black box is found, it will be taken to the maker of that plane to retrieve the information in the black box. So does it apply to human being. God is the sole maker of the soul and when you die, only God can retrieve the information from your soul. The soul is the recorder of your life, the black box, and when life terminates, God retrieves it to get full account of your life. Most of the things you are doing in the dark or doing at the private times you think no one is watching you, will be revealed on your judgment day. This "black box" which is inimitable, inexorable and has the memory that cannot be erased under any circumstance will be opened. "Life now is nothing but a race toward death, a race in which no one can stand still or slow down even for a moment."[44]

Have you imagined being in God's Court where your case would not need any further investigation and all your dirty secrets are revealed and used as evidence against you? The question would follow: "Are you guilty or not guilty?"

The person with a "guilty" verdict would hear: "Depart from me, you cursed, into everlasting fire, prepared for the devil and his demons" (Matthew 25: 41). This is a place no one wants to go, not even the wicked because it has endless misery, and the most inhospitable dwelling place where residents cry and gnaw their teeth on equal severity.

And the person with "not guilty" verdict would be told: "Come, you blessed of my Father, inherit the Kingdom prepared for you. ..." (Matthew 25:34). This is the City of God where the angels and saints enjoy perfect peace and tranquility. It is the highest and the greatest reward for those who have worked and prepared themselves positively for this opportunity of being given a permanent home and serenity of spirit. Most importantly, you will be out-of-reach for the devil, forever.

The judgment day is inevitable for every person and, it is better to retain an attorney in heaven by having the mother of God working with the angels and saints in heaven to intercede for you. If you would go to a distant place for the first time, would you not be happy having your loved ones waiting for you at the port of entry? When your flight leaves this earth going to God's Court which is the final destination of life, you cannot help yourself any more. The mother of God is not going to give excuses for your iniquities and mischievousness on earth, but to plead on your behalf for leniency. She will pray God for you to be adjudicated with kindness and for God to temper justice with mercy. The results are not guaranteed but the expectations are high. That's our faith as Christians.

We pray her to smoothen our ways and to reserve for us that eternal gift of salvation. We ask Her to be there for us until we are welcomed by her son Jesus. "The prayers of the Virgin Mary, in her Fiat and Magnificat, are characterized by the generous offering of her whole being in faith."[45]

SURRENDER TO GOD

W hen I was about seven years of age, my mother was seriously ill, and was not responding effectively to her medications. My father, without any doubt, was worried. My mother was expecting the worst to happen.

One day, I was alone with my sick mother in the house. She turned to me and said in a slow and soft voice: "if anything happens to me, make sure you take good care of your younger sister." I did not understand her message and I was afraid to ask my fragile sick mother for any clarification. I knew my mother was worried about her own condition but I never thought about anything happening to her for whatever reasons. The message did not make much meaning to me but I nodded my head in agreement. The inability to understand that my mother was talking about death made it difficulty to understand the message of taking care of my little sister if no other person was there. I could only rationalize about the family; my father, and my other big sister and two big brothers living in other states.

The best I knew about death then was that the person had gone to heaven. I remember being told at that age that my grand parents went to heaven. I didn't know they would stay there forever. I understood it to be a long distance journey and I expected they would come back after their trip.

Though my mother was seriously sick and could hardly speak, I expected her to recover. She had been sick several times in the past but not as serious as this one. she recovered after some days in every one of them. I had no reason to doubt of her recovering again.

I knew that three to four months before my mother got sick, I was sick myself. Nobody said that she got it from me but then, my parents took me to a catholic hospital about twenty miles away. I spent about one week there and I loved the hospital because they had a lot of nuns who were very nice to me. The day the doctor said I was going home because I was getting better, I didn't like to go. I was enjoying the attention I was getting from the nuns.

Finally, when we were about to depart from the hospital, one of the nuns touched my head, called my name and gave me a beautiful balloon. I was happy. When we got home, I told my mother and father that I would want to go back to that same hospital any time I got sick. My mother said: "sweetie, you are not going to get sick again." I didn't even know there was a hospital bill until I heard my parents talking about it. However, it wouldn't make any difference to me because I could not understand the value of money then.

I was surprised my mother was not taken to the same hospital when she was sick. Though accompanied by my father each time they were going to the doctor but, she was seeing a doctor few miles from our house. I expected to see those nuns again.

My father was an ardent Catholic, a prayer warrior, always saying his rosary every day and invested a lot of his time serving humanity and God. He believed particularly and in exceptional manner, in the intercession of Mary the mother of God. It was his conviction that we should appeal to her and present our concerns and sorrow to her; she will always convey them to her son. My father believed that any one without God in his or her life was like a grave decorated with beautiful flowers, which looks good on the outside but contains rotten materials in the inside. T. Keller explains it: "Without God, our sense of worth may seem solid on the surface, but it never is - it can desert you in a moment."[46]

My mother got better with time until she was able to continue with her normal duties. Pope John Paul II prayed and requested that those who are tried by sickness should unite the oblation of their suffering and keep the faith.[47] And St. James, the servant of Christ told us that the prayer of faith shall save the sick, and the Lord shall raise him up; and if he hath committed sins, they shall be forgiven him (James 5: 15).

The challenges of the world can, at times be over-whelming. We understand that we cannot do it alone. At the moments you hit the bottom and the spirit is weary, and the flesh disintegrates and seemed to be crippled, keeping to your faith, you will notice that the Holy Spirit helps you with your daily problems and in your praying. For you don't even know what you would pray for, but the Holy Spirit prays for you with such feelings that it cannot be expressed in words (Romans 8 : 26).

Heaven is the ultimate destination for everybody but the means to get there makes all the difference; things that happen along the way will determine if you will get to your destination or not. A pregnant woman goes through rough moments; at times, she entertains the fear of her life, but the safe arrival of the new baby wipes-out all the previous pains and trauma. " [W]hen it comes to goal pursuit, it really is the journey that counts, not the destination. ... Most of the pleasure will be had along the way, with every step that takes you closer."[48]

We also pray through songs. This is a song that gives me tears each time the choir sings it in the church; it gives me the opportunity to make a total surrender to God, praying him to take me, all I have, all I will have, my undivided attention, my dreams and sanctify them.

<u>Take and Sanctify</u>

Chorus:
Take and sanctify
For Your honor Lord,
And sanctify these gifts.
Take and sanctify these gifts
For your honor Lord.

1. All that I am, all that I do
Everything I will ever make
Take my life and take my all,
Everything I will ever make.

2. All that I need, all that I pray,
   Everything I will ever have
   Take my life and take my all,
   Everything I will ever have.

3. All that I dream, all that I crave
   Everything I will ever be
   Take my life and take my all
   Everything I will ever be.

4. Take our bread, we ask you;
   Take our hearts, we love you
   Take our lives, O Father,
   We are yours, we are yours.[49]

CHALLENGE OUR HOPE

The most amazing thing about life challenges is that there is no silver bullet to stopping the endless human problems which have no schedule or calendar. The only comforting solution, or the greatest gift which matters most in our lives is the gift of strength to be able to complete this marathon on earth and to expect a relaxed life in the world to come.

A lot of times when circumstances overflow beyond your control, or your life is sprinkled with challenges, if the future starts looking cloudy and foggy like you are not going to make it, or worse, when you have broken heart, frustration, abandonment, and nothing mattered to you, life will be blank. There are moments that after doing all you think you are supposed to do in life, you still find yourself walking on a thinly wire and having sporadic incidents that shake your faith and sanity; you keep asking: "are we there yet?" You re-examine yourself and your faith and you don't know what you could have done differently. David was in such a situation when he called God: "My tears have been my meat day and night, while [my enemies] continually say unto me, where is your God?" There are difficult circumstances of life that could come your way, and trying to disengage your feelings in order to survive it would seem difficult, even thinking to stay asleep than dealing with the reality would be unsatisfying, and awkward.[50]

There was a man, I call here, Joe; he wanted to give his two children the opportunity to acquire the best education the family could afford. He had been blessed by fortune. He sent them to a distant school away from his state. They traveled by air to and from their school than going by road that took many hours. These boys were among the brightest in their school. Joe and his wife were very proud of them.

During one of the holidays, the boys were flying home. Their father was waiting for them at the airport. Unfortunately, their plane which had reached the airport lost control on landing and busted into flames. Before the fire could be put off, all the passengers were burnt - there were no survivals. Joe lost his two children on this flight. His world was turned upside down.

Another tragedy was about my friend, Chris, as I fondly called him. He was a noble, affectionate and dear friend who had been there for other people in times of difficulty and in good times too. He took other peoples problems as his and tried to find solutions. I have seen him making great sacrifices for individuals that could not help themselves. He spent his savings for other people without asking for a refund or reward. He wasn't doing those things to impress any person but, because he had the good heart to help and share their feelings.

One day, the unexpected happened. Chris came home from a Baby-Shower he and his wife sponsored for a relation of his.

He was cheerful and funny throughout the party. He reached-out to all his guests and made sure every one was comfortable. There were a lot of food and drink, and the DJ was fabulous. People really had a good time and the expectant mother received numerous gifts. At the end of the party, Chris and his wife were thankful for the successful event.

Chris spent more time after the party helping to put things together, including the leftover bottles of wine, beer and other drinks. After the hard work, he left with members of his family. It was a busy evening, and Chris had to travel another twenty miles back home.

It was obvious that he would feel tired when he got home, so it wasn't a surprise when he slumped onto his couch as he got into the living room. His wife who was busy with other things they brought home, didn't notice that something was wrong until Chris complained of shortness-of-breath. His wife and other family member with them instantly called for emergency support. He was rushed to the nearest hospital which was less than three miles from his house.

On the Ambulance to the hospital's emergency room, and within that short ride, my friend's health deteriorated so rapidly that he was in a coma on arrival. All procedural efforts could not yield any good results. Family members, friends and well wishers jumped into frenzy prayers, begging for a divine intervention. Prayer warriors challenged their faith and God because they did not want to loose such a good man. After three years and three months of fasting and praying by different groups of people, relations, friends, and loved ones, he died. Everyone was left with tears, frustration and agony. His death became an agent of change as some faithful morphed into a spiritual eclipse.

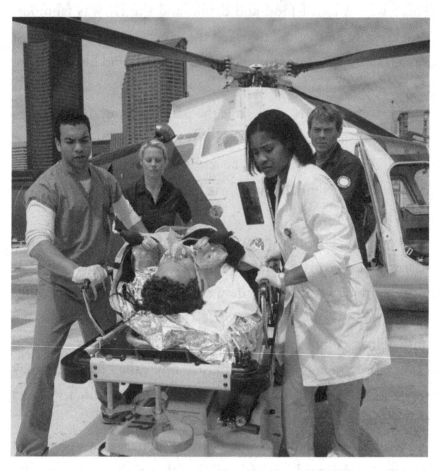

A moment of desperation in life.

"Pain can devour our spiritual sensibilities in the flames of disappointment, sadness, anger and despair. In moments of suffering, seconds turn into hours, hours turn into months .. of struggle to survive the creative whims of evil that challenge our hope in the promises of God."[51]

Does it mean that God was ignoring all this people for three years and three months? What has he done to be consumed by God's anger at his early age? Friends and loved ones fasted and prayed in vain for a divine mercy. Didn't God promise Abraham that he would not destroy a city because of ten people? (Gen. 18: 33). What about the innocent children and good ones who prayed on this man's behalf?

It was hard to believe he was gone. Friends and well wishers were asking: "why him?" His wife and family members were asking God why abandoning them when they needed Him most. As if the tragedy was not enough, and while the poor widow still had tears in her eyes, her mother died. There were so many unanswerable whys.

"...As we wait to leave [this world], having affection for others, having true and deep friendship with some human being, ...can make this fleeting life bearable and even enjoyable indeed that sometimes we don't want to leave even though we know that this is not our permanent home."[52]

All the uncountable "why him? Why now?" Tears and exclamation could not make any difference. There are moments in life when your expectations seemed to have roughened your faith, slammed the door on your face and struck you like a lightning. When every door seemed to be closed, and your world darkened; you ask yourself: "where is my God?" When you're weary and bitter about life, you will leave many complaints to yourself; mostly when it seems that expectations of help or rescue have vanished and tomorrow seemed to be on the rainy side. During this difficult times, judgmentalism should be abandoned because it causes the disease of the mind which torments and arouses sick emotions.

Sometimes we have difficulties controlling the immature qualities in us when we hurt and cry, because fear and concern cannot stop death. Irrespective of our unresolved bitterness, we cannot allow things of the world to be the ultimate love of our lives, otherwise God becomes licentious. "The more [you] identif[y] with God, the more will [you] be identified with all the others who are identified with Him."[53]

There was an amazing story about a boy, Sam, and his stormy journey to accomplish his vocation. He came from a very humble family. His parents could not afford to pay for his education. They loved him so much but had difficulties taking care of him and his siblings. Sam understood his parents' predicaments. It was not a sudden disaster but an existing low social status problem which he understood early in life. He was happy with himself and exercised self confidence irrespective of the family's economic problems. It was a Christian family who believed that "tomorrow would be better." Sam was prominent in the church, being an alter boy and an active member of some of the prayer groups.

One day, a Nun was fascinated with the intelligence and humility of this boy. She saw the shinning star in him and took over his education. It was through this benevolence that Sam was able to find his vocation to work for God. She sent him to seminary where he stayed in the boarding school. "God planted some people on your journey to prosperity and has planted you on other people's path to growth and abundance. You are path of a circle life of giving and receiving and you have a duty to do your part."[54]

Everything was going well, academically and otherwise for Sam, and he was very happy. His parents were grateful to the Nun for her support, and happy for their son for being a lucky person. He was looking forward to graduating from the seminary and becoming an ordained priest.

The devil is every where trying to disrupt the good work of God. One night, the director of the seminary boarding house was going around, supervising the night activities as a normal routine. He walked into Sam's dormitory. Each of the little hall was big enough to accommodate six to eight students. Without suspecting anything, there was a sudden darkness in the hall. Though Sam was standing close to one of the light switches, it was not from him. One of the students had mischievously switched off the light. No one knew who did it. The manner it happened indicated it was not by accident. One of the students was playing a prank but such little pranks on a school administrator in a seminary was completely unacceptable.

During the investigation to identify the culprit, three boys, for unknown motives, conspired and falsely accused Sam as the person. The result was clear. Sam was expelled from the seminary. The administrators were disappointed because he had been a bright student. The benefactor nun who wanted a better future for Sam was disappointed, presumably, for being involved in such a disrespectful behavior.

Sam knew he was innocent but had no way to prove himself right against three people testifying against him. Many other students were not sure what happened and could not give any useful information. His school mates knew he was a playful person in the seminary but not mischievous. It was certain to him that his dismissal would be the end of his educational pursuit and end of his hope of attaining a good life. His life ambitions were no more within his reach. He wept over it and left when he was notified by the Rector to go. He could not understand why God would allow such thing to happen to people like him.

He lost hope in every thing except prayer. His sole ambition in life was to serve God. He continued to ask God why he was rejected in such a shameful manner. There was no doubt that his life became more difficult than any person could imagine. His benefactor backed-off and his parents could not afford sending him to another school.

"Having a steadfast faith in God does not guarantee a happy, carefree life" said Dr. James Dobson. "On the contrary, our faith almost guarantees us some form of abuse from the world."[55] "When our present condition of suffering seems irreconcilable with the God of our faith - poses great spiritual difficulties as we seek meaning from God and listen for His response."[56]

After few months, and when Sam least expected that anything good would come his way, he got a letter from the Rector of the seminary. His hand trembled when he got the letter. He did not know what it was all about but imagined it could be a follow up letter about his dismissal. It took another round of rosary to get the courage to open the letter. He was being recalled to school unconditionally.

"To pass through toil and sweat, and to arrive at a good end, namely life, is sufficient solace to those who undergo these struggles. For sailors can make light of storms and soldiers of wounds in hope of perishable rewards, much more when Heaven lies before, and rewards immortal, will none look to the impending dangers."[57]

He jubilated over it but could not really guess what prompted the administration's change of heart. He even suspected that they wanted to give him a lesser punishment but the letter said it was an unconditional recall. Whatever the reason could be, recalling him to school was all he was asking God to do for him.

Sometimes in life, we encounter unexpected road detours, mostly when the road is not navigable. We travel through other connective avenues to return to our proper route. It's not new or strange to our daily endeavors. It is always a living truth that others can delay what God has for you but cannot stop it. And Monsignor Nwaorgu rightly revealed that life has a way of conspiring to throw in some discomforting obstacles into the mix of our lives.[58] When your feather is roughened, locking yourself up in your house and crying all day and night will not be close to solving your problem, but creates more pain and agony.

Having come back to school, he found that the three conspirators, the boys who lied against him, later quarreled among themselves for other reasons and spilled the truth to the school authority. All of the three were expelled from the seminary. Although Sam did not wish that to happen to them but he had no control over such outcome. He continued with his education, successfully concluded his junior and subsequent senior seminary education and became an ordained Priest.

No matter where the roller coaster of life takes you, you should be strong in the believe that a life not centered on God leads to emptiness. It is obvious that building your life on something besides God not only hurts you if you don't get the desires of your hearts, but also if you do.[59] In the pursuit of your spiritual growth, it is worth remembering this prayer:

"Lord, thou knowest what it is best; let this or that be according as thou wilt. Give what thou wilt, so much as thou wilt, when thou wilt. Do with me as thou knowest best, and as shall be most to thine honour. Place me where thou wilt, and freely work thy will with me in all things. ... When could it be evil when thou wert near? I had rather be poor for thy sake than rich without thee. I choose rather to be a pilgrim upon the earth with thee, than without thee to possess heaven. Where thou art, there is heaven; and where thou art not, behold there death and hell." [60]

Do not give up your faith even when you hit the bottom. Be prayerful. Never let the fear of fall becloud your ambition, we all fall at one point in life or another. Your zeal to rise should not go down with you. Raise your hand each time you fall, for your rescue may be closer than you know. God answers prayers in many forms; you never know which rescue squad is coming your way.

One of the mysteries of the Christian faith is to accept that when God had not intervened in your lives in the manners you asked from him and of the time you wait for him, it does not necessarily mean he was not listening to your request. Even when you're living illustriously, trying to fulfill wildest dreams, the failure to be rich, popular or achieving other immediate desires does not evidence that God is not listening. God gives you credit when he sees how hard you are trying to reach him, but Hugh Prather said: "life is a mixture of unsolved problems, ambiguous victories and vague defeats - with very few moments of clear peace."

It is natural to say that people treasure more the things they get through a hard way than through easy entitlements. A woman who has five children may not treasure all of them like the woman who spent five years working hard before getting one child. The later woman will pamper the only child as the most valuable treasure from God, while the other woman would love hers but will not have equal emotional attachments.

Fr. Sam has became a phenomenal priest. Only God knows what he wants him for and what He wants him to conquer but one thing is certain as St. Aquinas said: "Our love for God is proved to be much stronger, as the more difficult are the things we accomplish for its sake."[61] A French priest, M. Vianney who lived exemplary holy life once stated: "There is but one way in which to give one's self to God, - that is, to give one's self entirely, and to keep nothing for one's self. The little that one keeps is only good to trouble one and make one suffer."[62]

IN TIMES OF DISTRESS

//

When Job seemed to have hit the bottom of hopelessness and helplessness; when he thought both man and God had abandoned him, he said: "Oh, that I knew where to find God; that I could go to his throne and talk with Him there. I would tell Him all about my side of this argument, and listen to his reply, and understand what He wants." (Job: 23, 3- 5).

When Jesus was in the human form, he was humiliated and rejected, the Jews chose a criminal over him and asked their King, Pilate, to condemn Jesus to death for no just reasons, he was heavily burdened. Realizing the physical and emotional torture waiting for Him, He told His disciples that His Soul was crushed with horror and sadness (Matthew 26: 38). When He realized the suffering He was going to be subjected to, He fell on the ground and prayed: "Father! If this is possible, let this cup be taken away from me." (Matthew 26: 39). That was purely a natural human reaction, the weakness of the flesh. Though, he voluntarily took a human form, to interact with humans and to cleanse their delinquencies, but he reached a point he was overwhelmed and battered by affliction and vicissitudes of this life, he cried to his Father: "My God, why have thou forsaken me?" (Matthew 27: 46, Mark 15: 34). A cry of the wounded, in desperation and urgency which is the routine of life here on earth.

But, Jesus refused to give-up. As Augustine explained it: "We are to use the world, not with the love and delight we would show to our true home, but only with the passing love we would give a highway or vehicle of travel. We love the things that carry us only because we love the place to which they carry us."[63]

There was also a time when Moses found himself in such a distressful situation. The Israelites were displeased with his leadership and they complained about their suffering and Moses' inability in providing answers to their problems. He could not sustain the pressure on him and he called God: "I am not able to bear all this people alone, because it is too heavy for me" (Numbers 11: 14).

Although Moses could not bear the burden of his people any further, but he continued to pray to God to control his anger against the Israelites. "Pardon, I beseech thee, the iniquity of this people according unto the greatness of thy mercy, and as thou hast forgiven this people, from Egypt even until now." Moses did not abandon his position or told God he was quitting, but he asked for support and compassion.

It is the distress of sickness, pain, agony, disappointments, poverty, failures and death that human beings can not get over with - just abuse from the world as Dr. Dobson explained. "With suffering, there are no escape clauses. Its sharp tendrils reach all of us and cut deeply."[64]

There was a story of a kidney transplant patient who was in the surgery room hoping to get his transplant; both the medical team and the patient were ready and about to start. Unfortunately, it was realized within few minutes that a nurse who was in the surgery room earlier, preparing things for the surgery, saw the cooler and did not know that the kidney was still there, accidentally threw away everything in the cooler with ice, thinking it was all ice. When the mistake was realized, it was late to save the organ. It was an unprecedented medical error but the damage had been done. The patient was wheeled out to wait for another opportunity for an organ donor. Wailings and tears could not be controlled for the lost opportunity. How could this happen? Why?

When Eli was told that God was going to punish him because of the iniquities of his children which he knew but did not stop, he replied: "It is the Lord, let him do what he thinks best" (1 Samuel 3:18).

When natural obstacles seem to be insurmountable.

Incomplete Gift of God

//

I f you have been a family member of a person who has physical or mental challenges and getting therapeutic support from health agencies, you will get this picture clearer; when all kinds of therapists are flooding your house at different hours of the day and night, offering pieces of advise and various recommendations, everything in the name of therapeutic support, you would start wondering how long it would take getting over it all. You would resign yourself, if not frustrated when you understand it wouldn't go away soon.

It is very demanding living with children with neurological disorders, especially with autism. It takes a tremendous impact on the parents, guardians and the loved ones especially, causing them high levels of stress, and severity of pains seeking for solutions that are not available. It can be devastating and shattering at times, watching this little angels with intellectual disabilities, struggling with speeches, impulsivity, aggression and the inabilities to interact normally with other kids. The conditions are a lifelong issues although it may vary on the individuals. It is unbelievable how these beautiful kids can suffer so much in their lives time because nature did not tighten the loose ends.

I know a very handsome boy, a precious ornament of God, admired and adored by almost every person that saw him. If seen at his best moments, and if you looked into his blue eyes, you would think he was the most beautiful handwork of God.

Inwardly, he was something else, a volcano; not of his own design but imposed on him by creation. His anger and tantrum could erupt at any moment without any notice or any known cause. He could head-butt, scratch deep into your skin or bite you. He hit any person around him at some moments without minding the relationship. The monstrous outburst from within him would hurt people physically and emotionally. You would look at his face a few minutes later, and you'll think a different individual gave you the scars on you.

Yes, it was him. He would calm down in a few minutes and his angelic behavior would reappear. He would laugh and play like nothing happened. If you were the parents of this child, you would be tempted to yell, scream and ask God: "what type of incomplete gift is this?" "Why did you send [Your] best gift in such ugly wrappings?"[65]

There are certain times one's faith can be stretched to its elastic end by no person's fault. It is not every time the result would come out heroic like, when God asked Abraham to sacrifice his only son, Isaac. No one would want to be put in such a difficult position that would give deep traumatic experience.

Look at this intriguing apprehension of an electrical contractor who was called to repair a power problem at the lion den part of a zoo. Due to this power problem, the area was closed to the public. The zoo keepers were inside the building, possibly cleaning up while the lions were outside.

The electrician climbed up the high electric pole to fix the wires. As he climbed up through the back fence, and before connecting his safety belt to the pole, he slipped from his ladder and lost his balance. Fortunately, he caught one of the dead wire lines he had turned off before climbing to work on them.

The lions didn't know what was really happening but they kept walking around the vicinity, looking up toward him. He screamed: "Lord! Please help!!"

He instantly heard a voice which asked him what he wanted. He replied again: "Lord save me!"

The voice responded again: "Leave your hands and I will catch you below." He looked down and saw the lions still looking at him, he screamed again: "where are the zoo keepers?" There were only three lions at the place but they seemed to him like a hundred of them; though one lion was dangerous enough.

You can remember how many times it has passed through your mind that God abandoned you when you needed him most. You are not alone. Many other people ask the same question at various circumstances like Martha the sister of Lazarus: "Lord, if you had been there, my brother wouldn't have died..." (John 11:21). And, many other people that would tell God: "If you had answered my prayers, I wouldn't have been in this precarious situation; if you had heard my cries, my only child would not have died; if you had listened to me, this disaster in my family would not have happened; if you had seen my tears, I wouldn't have been barren; this is a God fearing community, if you had been our God this calamity would not have happened to us;" and on and on.

Crossing through the unpleasant path of life.

"Is it possible to find joy as we toss and turn on the unmade lumpy bed that is our life just now?"[66] There are many hard questions to ask when we experience the life's storms and tribulations. One of the few answers from thoughtful minds said: "Probably because it was intended by God that all pain should end in this earth."[67] The assessment of the relative value is that we will have the capacity to exhaust all pain and sorrows here on earth as to be able to acquire our reserved places in heaven. "The sorrows of this life are not worthy to be compared with the joys that are to come."[68] Augustine describes heaven's life as abstaining from the quirks, foibles, and small irrational attachments of human life in this world. "The life described is one fit only for heroes - but promised to all."[69]

No matter where and how we find ourselves at any time, we should praise and worship God. "[W]e have to be grateful [to God]," said Prof. Nwankwo, "regardless of the bumps."[70] This is the primary reason why we are created. We are made to love, worship and praise God all the days of our lives. All creatures obey this conduct. Human beings have more responsibility to God because when the earth was created, God gave man knowledge and put him in-charge of his massive of creation.

Leadership comes with commitments: leadership in our families, places of work and in dealing with other vicissitude of life. Interestingly, no matter how many people are in a car, there is only one driver's seat and one driver at a time.

The challenge in the process of exercising your leadership duties may have some consequences. It may stir some pressure, stress and emotion. The ability to handle or overcome these challenges may depend on your preparedness to confront them. Even when you as human beings are not prepared, God gave you a backup - prayer. "Ask and it will be given to you." Because of the leadership position God had granted man from the garden of Eden, human beings are more protected than other creatures, because other creatures were not given the kind of knowledge and wisdom that human beings have.

Coping with Disasters

///

One day I was at a Park and all the trees were shaking and some of them whistling because it was windy. I saw a beautiful bird's nest on the ground. It caught my attention because of what seemed to be a professionally descent weaving. I spent a good time looking and admiring the nest. It was not my first time seeing a bird's nest, but one could hardly pass this very one without a glance. I began to observe closely the makeup of the nest. I saw over a thousand pieces of dry grasses, leaves and cotton-like materials.

Knowing how birds pick things in small pieces, it came to my mind that the bird-owner of that nest must have flown over a thousand trips from the top of whichever tree it was, to the field and wood where it collected those nest-building materials. The labor of weaving and decorating the nest must have taken countless hours.

The bird did not give up until the nest was completed. It must have complimented itself when it was finished and it saw the beauty of its work, and probably said: "I have fought a good fight, I have finished my course, I have kept faith ..." now awaits the reward of my labor, (2 Timothy 4: 7 - 8) to enjoy its nest.

It won't be a selfish expectation to have a lasting joy after all the efforts. I don't know how long the bird had enjoyed its newly built home, but it didn't seem long judging from how new and fresh some parts of the nest looked like. After all the hard labor, the wind blew the nest away - natural disaster.

How would any person feel being in the bird's shoes. Devastating? Heartbreaking? But, the bird wasn't exactly that way. I saw some birds perching on one of the trees, may be nest-less but singing, and I knew the bird-owner of the lost nest would be among the ones singing, and probably praising God. The birds sing and rejoice at all times, and "when they perceive that they must die, mostly swan, having sung all their life long, [they] then sing more than ever, rejoicing in the thought that they are about to go away to the [G]od whose ministers they are."[71] We, human beings are more dramatic with our traumatic encounters.

Faith is the acceptability and conviction that the impossible will be possible without seeing it. We hoped for it but have not seen it (Hebrew 5:1). It was faith that motivated Abel to make the good sacrifices to God; Noah built an ark and Abraham tried to sacrifice his only son, Isaac, to God; the crossing of the Israelite through the Red Sea, (Hebrew 11: 2 - 40); the birth of Christ through Virgin Mary, his resurrection and many other wonders from God.

Walk in faith and whole-heartedly trust yourself unto Him and believe that though you walk through the value of death that no evil will happen to you because He will protect and comfort you (Psalm 23: 4). Without faith, you will live in fears, over-powered by your adversaries and subdued.

Look at what happened to Peter when he saw Christ walking on the water, having the confidence and conviction of faith, he asked to walk like Christ on the water. Christ responded in the positive: "Come!" Peter walked on water but when his faith wavered, he began to sink. (Matt. 14: 25 - 31).

HOPE AND HELP

//

L ife is full of wonders. It is said that wonder lies in the experience that the world is more profound, more commodious, more mysterious than it appears to our everyday understanding.[72] The only last resort for the child of God is to hang on in your faith so that, at the end of the sojourn, you will have a better life in the world to come.

Never wish your life to be like any other. If there are things you found lacking in your life, work it out with God. Though, there may be moments you will find yourself in such an incredible stress, loosing your baseline and thinking you are in the worst situation than any living human being, when you will be consumed by fear and anxiety because you think you have reached the dead-end of any good expectations, without knowing that some of this problems are temporary. You may think that some people comfortably glide through life, but you may never know where the roller coaster of life took them. It may be a shocker to know that you have had better days than them.

It is hard to move on
when faced with frustrating predicaments.

William had been married for over five years to his school sweet heart whom he used to call "Love of my life." The couple had been quarrelling and fighting a lot in the last few years. The love that held them together could not hold on any more as William complained that his wife was not respecting him in the house.

In the recent time, the couple could not agree on anything any more: from children's issues to money and about their extended family members. Now they have diverse opinions on everything. These two individuals were inseparable before they got married, but have started sleeping in their different beds.

One day, they quarreled so much that William's wife called him a foolish man and made other nasty statements. He called his wife the enemy of his life. William was so upset and could not get over his wife's comment.

He left a few hours later to report his wife to their Godfather/ mother who had been counseling them in similar situations. He respected the couples a lot, considering them to be very peaceful people, and that impression of them motivated him going to them in times of crisis for support. As he got closer to their house, he heard someone crying but wasn't sure where it was coming from. When he got to the door and was about to knock, he heard loud voices of arguments coming from inside the house.

He held his breath. He heard things crashing in the house, and his Godfather was calling his Godmother an idiot. He tiptoed backward and left in amazement that the people he thought had perfect marriage could also quarrel. He returned home and resolved his problems with his wife telling her that he realized that among every marriage couple, one is either foolish or an idiot.

I met a friend I have not seen in over five years. He was driving a late model car, well dressed up and sported a nice pair of shoes. I flattered him about his dressing and jokingly said to him: "when I grow up, I would be like you."

He looked at my face, chuckled for a few seconds before replying: "Please, Please, don't be like me because if you are like me, you would cry!"

There was a physician on the news who used to work in the emergency unit of a hospital; she was once the physician of the year in the country. One day, she was involved in a very serious car accident. She crashed her car onto another car that caused cracked ribs and a hematoma on the leg of a 78 year old driver of the other car. Every indication about the accident seemed to be pointing against her.

During the cause of the police investigation, it was found that the physician was on controlled substance, and more were found in her car. Her attorney said that she had some personal problems. Though the victim of the accident said he was hammered by the impact of the crash, but he said that he had no grudges against the "poor woman (who) probably got more problems than I'll ever have, so let it go with that."[73]

There must have been people who saw this person as a role model in the past or had wished to be like this physician that worked in an emergency unit. There is no doubt that some of the peers must have desired being the liked physician of the year but, none of these people knew about others personal problems that spilled over to cause the catastrophe on the high way. Be careful what you ask for because you may get it, and it may not be pleasant.

Many times, it seems that we put ourselves in the situation that squeeze blood out of our nerves because of desperation and ideation. We put ourselves in the positions we can hardly come of it and start blaming God for allowing those things to happen. People make wrong turns by resorting to illusionary solutions and by getting involved in drugs or alcohol or both. Most often, the individual will start dwelling in thwarted hopes and dreams, and continue with feelings of defeat.

There are certain times you miss the rescue squad God sends to you because you overlook them. God opens your eyes for you to find what you are looking for, but most of the time, you don't take the advantage.

Jackson lost his job when the economy was getting bad. He could not get another job and he began to borrow money from friends to pay some bills. One day Jackson thought he had reached his breaking point because of the overwhelming difficulty coming his way; he became depressed and started planning on how to take his own life. As he was about to execute his plan, his phone rang. He didn't even remember that he had the phone by his side. At first, he didn't want to answer the call but reluctantly picked it up.

It was his good friend who saw a job opportunity at his place of work and wanted Jackson to apply. Jackson did not tell his friend he was about committing suicide but that call disrupted his effort. After the conversation with his friend, he started having the feelings that there are people who think good of him, and such people could have been disappointed if he had died. His sense of balance was restored.

The angel of God does not necessarily come to people in white robes. God does not always answer people's prayers by calling from heaven or appearing as he did to Moses, Isaac, Jacob,

Abraham, Solomon and others. It could happen, He is the God of Yesterday, Today and Tomorrow. However, "[b]e not forgetful to entertain strangers: for thereby some have entertained angels unawares." (Hebrew 13:2).

One of my friends used to joke that if you are going to church and on your way you find a new bible, if nobody comes for it, God is telling you to keep and read it. You don't need another angel to bring that message to you.

Despite all other things God has been doing for you, waking you up every day is a miracle. Life is a gift because you don't own it, and each day you get it is a miracle and you should be appreciative. Go to the hospitals, especially, the emergency rooms and see how people arrived at the hospital, or woke up from their sleep, or how they completed their day. Some of them are on feeding tubes, others on breathing machines, or have lost limbs, or suffering from other chronic sicknesses. There are many who did not wake-up. Compare all these situations to what God has done for you. Look around you, there must be a blessing God has done for you. He did not leave anybody empty handed. I remember a childhood story which happened to be a reality: some people have food to feed themselves but are sick and lack the appetite to eat, and there are others who have good appetite to eat but cannot afford the food; for those who have the food and the appetite to eat should be thankful to God.

I have had countless miracles in my life but the most prominent one happened when I was a student in Sao Paulo. I was a full time student and could not work. There wasn't any regular means of income than on the benevolence of others. One particular month, I had no money for my house rent. My period of grace to make my payment had passed and I could not come up with the money.

I was close to becoming homeless because I was about to be evicted by the Landlord. I had no person I could go to for help. Whenever I saw any person coming towards my address during the day, I started thinking I was being served with the eviction notice. I could only have rest of mind during the night that I knew the offices were closed. As my hope to come up with the rent waned, I trembled.

It was almost impossible to focus on my academic assignments as a daily meal was almost becoming a luxury to me. I still had little money to buy few loaves of bread; at times, it was a choice between buying the bread and being able to pay for my transportation to the university for classes. A very hard choice to contemplate about.

Something inside me told me to be strong, but I could not understand how I would be strong under such circumstances I had. It seemed like my education and my world were crumbling before me. I was a stranger, and my only relation in the country was a cousin who was also a student but lived far away from me. He was in no condition to help because he was also hanging on the string of his survival.

One desperate evening, I walked out to the street without having any destination in mind. About fifty yards away from my residence, I used a coin I found in my pocket and called my cousin at the public phone booth. I was on the call and making jokes with my cousin, and did not notice when someone came behind me and tapped on my shoulder. I startled, without knowing what I was really thinking about by then.

He was a business man, a friend of mine from Nigeria that I had not seen for a long time. He came on a business trip, lodged in a hotel and felt like stopping over to see me. He was not really sure I was still living at that same address but wanted to try.

He got to the address and did not see me but saw a door mat he suspected could belong to me. He began to think I could still be living there. He did not want to give up but wanted to make one more attempt of finding me before going back to his hotel. Again, it was the only day he could come out before getting on with his business.

He walked some yards down the street to see if I went to any nearby store. As he was walking down the street, he found me talking at the public pay phone. It was a big excitement seeing each other.

We went back to my house and he quickly found out that I had nothing to eat at home. He inquired, and I unloaded all my episode to him. He was subdued by emotion. He put his hand on my shoulder, feeling sorry for me. I was swept off my feet when he took me to the food store to buy food for me, he also took me to my Landlord and paid my rent.

I was like Lazarus rising from the dead. I could not contain my gratification though I was worried about the amount of money he spent on me. I knew he was an average business man, and I did not know how the expenses on me would affect his business transaction during the trip. But, his presence alone at that moment of my life was really a mystery. "We live among mysteries. The mysteries of change; ... the mysteries of identity. Both are realities, but inseparable realities."[74]

Faith is the only link between Human Being and Heaven. "The value of faith cannot be explained, even though efforts are often made to do so, by merely stressing its usefulness for human morality."[75]

It is difficult to untangle the intricacies and mysteries of God's response to human behaviors. Faith is the only answer why we should not give up hope and help. God's silence does not necessarily mean a rejection. He is the Alpha and Omega and His time is not our time. He works only on His own schedule.

If you are a parent, there are certain things you cannot give your child no matter how serious he/she asks for it. If you know or think that such thing is not for the best interest of the child, you cannot grant the child his/her request. Knife is good depending, who is using it and what he is using it for. It is of great significance to know that, one of the most important things a child must learn is that emotions are not adequate guides to action.[76]

Each time we pray, it is a complete review of our conscience and also the re-fortress of our position against our adversary. It is a bold claim of our God's importance and a manifestation of his power, and reminder that help is on the way, without minding if the help would come in timely manners. We need a lot of prayers for sustenance through our human challenges and fragility, and to over-come the confrontations through the vicissitude of life.

THE NARROW GATE
TO HEAVEN

The gate to Heaven, the entrance to the ultimate place for eternal peace and infinite love of God, is narrow; going through all the crucibles of life slims you down in part preparation to get to the finish line. There has been an analogy that God allows the sheets on our bed to be wrinkled so that we will not fall in love with this earthly stable instead of longing for the true home that awaits us in heaven.[77]

When we fall in love with the wealth of the world instead of the wealth of God, the gate of heaven gets narrower. The wealth of the world and humility are never in good combination. The wealth of the world goes with arrogance, power, insubordination and vindictiveness. It is a big and heavy baggage that cannot go through the narrow gate of heaven. If your possession is good for the services of God, they are acceptable and beautiful. "But no matter how beautiful created nature is, it can become the focus for wrongful loves that lead people away from God."[78]

If you want to be an angel, you have to be angelic. If you want to be a President, you have to look presidential. We can not keep doing the things that will block our access to heaven because of temporary comfort on earth. Candy is sweet but too much of it ruins your digestion; you may end up in the hospital or die. "[L]ife is not just about successful becoming here on earth; there is also a greater need for successful arrival into eternity."[79]

A rich man came to Jesus and asked what he would do to enter into heaven; Jesus gave him all the commandments he was supposed to keep. The rich man replied that he knew all that and had kept all the commandments, and Jesus told him: "Sell all you have, give them to the poor and you will have treasure in heaven: come and follow me."

That was too hard for him to swallow. The rich man did not only remember all his wealth which he would give away, but the thought about the life of the poor he would live when all his wealth was gone. The man considered "the ordinary consequence and effects of poverty, which are hunger, thirst, cold, fatigue, and the denudation of all conveniences,"[80] he was sorrowful and walked away. (Matthew 19:16 - 22). He forgot what Christ said: "Blessed are you poor: for yours is the kingdom of God. Blessed are you who are now hungry: for you shall be satisfied. Blessed are you that weep now: for you shall laugh." (Luke 6: 20 - 21). Paul clarified it in his letter to his church when he said: "You know how full of love and kindness our Lord Jesus Christ was: though he was very rich, yet to help you he became very poor, so that by being poor he could make you rich." (2 Corinthians 8:9). Augustine explains it that the path to personal salvation lies through a future of personal self-abnegation in the love of God and of neighbor. "Paradoxically, to save one's soul means abandoning all morbid preoccupation with self by immersion in self effacing love."[81]

A practical revelation came from Simon the fisherman; fishing was his means of livelihood. One day, he fished all night and caught barely nothing. He helped Jesus when people were pressing on him and Jesus wanted to borrow Simon's boat to push out a little into the water to speak to the crowd. After preaching to the crowd, Jesus wanted to reward Simon for his kindness. Though he knew that Simon could not catch any fish all night, he asked Simon to cast his net back to the water; Simon explained his experience through the night but obeyed Jesus to satisfy his desire. Dramatically, the cast caught so much fish that needed support from partners at another boat to bring them out from the water. Both Simon's boat and the other boat were filled with fish and on the verge of sinking. James and John who witnessed this event were amazed.

Simon was astonished, and was regaining himself from the thrilled experienced when Jesus asked him to abandon all the fish and boats, and to follow Him. "You would be a fisher of men," He told Simon. The immediate challenge was enormous because Simon depended on fishing for his livelihood. Surprisingly, and without any hesitations, Simon brought his ship to the land, forsook all, and followed Jesus (Luke 5: 1- 11).

Jesus told his followers that it is hard for a rich man to enter into heaven. He did not say that a rich man cannot or will never enter into heaven, but the edifice of the narration was on the material distraction, the slip and fall that the worldly wealth could cause. As Jesus was sending out his disciples to villages and towns, he warned them not to go with money or to be asking for money and carrying purse; (Luke 10:1 - 4) only to be humble and selfless to people. He assured that they will not lack their daily bread. The premise of the message is to pronounce yourself the vows of poverty, chastity and obedience; the direct way of accepting the cross.

Jesus did not promise his disciples that life would be easy for them rather, he highlighted that they were going like lambs among wolves; (Luke 10: 3) he lay it out and was building their spirit and strength against the dangers ahead of them: the risk of being killed or thrown into jail for his name. You will also be challenged with the inclination of succumbing to different forms of manipulation and exploitation of man.[82] "Men are so simple of mind, and so much dominated by their immediate needs, that a deceitful man will always find plenty who are ready to be deceived."[83]

The services of God and the entire life journey of man have been rough and need focus. There are a lot of slippery grounds and Jesus knew the disciples would need a lot of courage and strong will to bear the challenges when the going is tough. It is the profound determination that gives the resistance and ability to pronounce that even at the point of death, that if such is the will of God that you are willing.[84] Again, we learnt that in the great spiritual community of the lovers of God it is possible to offer up pain and suffering in order that others who lack love of God may find it through others' efforts. "That is reparation."[85]

OUR SALVATION

///

What do we do with our faith? We use our faith to carry our petition to God. We talk and have conversation with God. It is prayer. "Prayer is an opportunity to let in what would otherwise be left out. Air is there if we breathe, light is there if we open our eyes, and the gifts we receive from Heaven depend on our trust."[86]

It is true that God knows all our problems and has all the solutions to our problems, but it is our responsibility to demonstrate our disposition and grace to let God in to help. Giving gift to someone who doesn't want it, or would not appreciate it is not of moral goodness. Putting a gold on dog does not make any sense because the dog will not appreciate its value.

"Commit everything you do to the Lord. Trust Him to help you do it and He will." (Psalm 37:5). You can not go to God in pretence nor can you make a wrongful claim. You cannot go to Him with obscure mind. You must tell Him all you want with humility, clear and calm mind. The next step is to consider whether you are making a reasonable request; if you ask for something that will not be of good interest to you, he will not give it to you no matter how hard you cry about it.

Sometimes, consciously or not, we demand things that may be harmful to us at the short or long run. There must have been a time in your life when you prayed for something and did not get it; but later in life, you found out that what you asked for could not have been of any good to you; you thanked God for not giving it to you. Haven't you heard the saying that every disappointment from God is a blessing?

Pope John Paul II said that we must recognize humbly and realistically that we are poor creatures, confused in our ideas, tempted to evil, frail and weak, continually in need of inner strength and comfort.[87] The only way to approach God is by being comfortable with Him. "Be joyful and gladdened in your interior recollection with Him, for you have Him so close to you. Desire him there, adore him there. Do not go in pursuit of him outside yourself. You will only become distracted and wearied thereby, and you shall not find him ..."[88]

A lot of times, we exaggerate our expectations, demands and desires. We do not present our cases properly to God and when we do, we could not listen adequately to his response. While there is no easy answer to our problems and anticipations, our faith requires that we have our eyes on the ball, Jesus Christ. Keep waiting for him and trusting in him no matter how long his silence to you may last. "Commit thy way unto the Lord; trust also in him; and he shall bring it to pass." (Psalm 37: 5)

I went to an auto work shop of a friend of mine, Iroko; I saw a book on the table at the waiting room titled "I am Second"[89] with a picture of a man tattooed all over his body with a long braided hair. Out of curiosity, I picked up the book and opened the content page. I saw this caption: "If Tomorrow Never Comes"[90] I wondered what it could be. It was hard to drop this book as I wanted to know more about the Tomorrow story.

It was a fascinating story from Tamara who was narrating her experience with cancer. Her courage, strength, and faith to fight this serious sickness were phenomenal. "Augustine believed that even though the Christian martyrs chose death, they did not cease to love life."[91]

When Tamara was first notified of the cancer which her doctor said had spread over 90 percent of her body, she was saddened and almost melted like ice in a hot weather. But with her fortitude in faith to confront this monstrous disease, she said: "[t]here were still battles to face, but having a relationship with God meant that there was always someone to lean on."[92]

After all that went through her thoughts and mind, mostly leaving her relatives, friends and all the loved ones so early in life, considering that she hadn't done anything to deserve being put through this debilitating agony, she paused and calmed down. After being at peace with herself, she accepted the portentous challenge instead of shrieking and groaning mostly, after the chemotherapy, pains and vomiting and other side effects of her medications. She later explained: "I never heard God say to me I was going to be healed or anything, but I knew that in some way He was going to be with me through it all."[93]

Her faith sustained her and some miracles happened in her life, the cancer disappeared. However, God's solution to our earthly problems is basic and temporary. There is no permanent solution. Until we meet with him in heaven, there is no end to our problems. "Come unto me, all ye that labor and are heavy laden, and I will give you rest." (Matthew 11: 28). That's all He promised. He did not assure to eliminate our problems permanently, but to give only a break. The length of this interruption to your burden will depend on your personal relationship with God. When you present your petition properly to God, you will be bailed out of your case. This does not mean that you have been discharged or acquitted - your case is not over; it is still pending. Heaven is the only place we are promised eternal peace and rest. That is the only place things are permanent.

PEACE

P eace is the greatest gift of God. It is the most important security we have in human lives. There can be no progress in any thing we do without peace; whether it is in our private lives, families, places of work, school, or churches. You can never have too much of it. The more you have it, the better person you are.

When Jesus was preparing his disciples before his departure from the earth, He said to them: "Peace I leave to you, my peace I give unto you: not as the world giveth, give I unto you. Let not your heart be troubled, neither let it be afraid." (John. 14: 27).

It was a powerful gift and he assured them that it was not like the gifts of the world which are not genuine, and not secured, but a long lasting empowerment. This is a gift for safety and protection he had always given his people. "Open the gates to everyone, for all may enter who love the Lord. He will keep in perfect peace all those who trust in him, whose thoughts turn often to the Lord!" (Isaiah 26: 2- 3).

When Jesus was crucified and buried, his disciples were hopeless and helpless. They were confused and afraid that the enemies of Jesus would come after them. Some of them thought Jesus was powerful and was beyond human destruction; and some thought he would come down from the cross to fight the enemies, or would ask His Father to send thunder and lighting to annihilate them, and when none of those expectations happened, they felt defeated and disappointed.

Remember Peter who was even made the head of the church, though he showed some fortitude by following his master through the tough moments, but when he saw the guards with swords and arrows, and the dragging of Jesus whom he considered the unconquerable, he could not stand his ground. Peter was asked three times if he knew Jesus or was with him, having been overwhelmed by what Jesus was going through, he denied having anything to do with him. (Matthew 26: 69 - 73, Luke 22: 56 - 60).

It is obvious you cannot trust many of your friends in times of most need. Being there for your loved one both at the good time and the difficult time is supposed to be the essence of friendship. When your life starts getting rough and cranky, the people you consider to be your close associates would disperse, and avoid you. People you had hoped on because of the past relationship would disappoint you, and become distant friends. You would realize how fragile human beings would be in times of difficulties.

Peter and the other disciples saw their future challenged and punctured. They did not have the abilities to move on. No other leader was courageous enough to get them out of their crises. They were spiritually depressed , feeling incomplete, incredible fear and stress of revenge and persecution. It seemed like the end of their world.

While the disciples assembled at their hiding place, being in desperation and desolation, they lost the strength and spirit to persevere to the end. The messages and preparations Jesus had given them for this contingency, evaporated into the thin air. All the explanations that He had a relationship with His Father, most especially notifying them about his ability to rise on the third day, none of them was assimilated. Even when He explained to them: "And I say unto you my friends, be not afraid of them that kill the body, but have no power over the soul. But I tell you whom to fear - fear God who has power to kill and cast into hell" (Luke 12: 4 - 5). Jesus also made it clear that He came to fulfill the prophesy: "Yes, it is written long ago that Christ must suffer and die and rise again from the dead on the third day..." (Luke 24: 46).

Fear consumed the disciples and they were terrified to come out. In midst of this agony and abandonment, behold Jesus appeared before them and said: *"Peace be unto you."* (John 20:19).

Jesus could have said to them: "Cheers! Be Happy! I am here again!" But he chose to give them the ammunition to fight their future battle; *"Peace be unto you"* I am sending you out as my Father sent me to you. It sounded good that Jesus was sending them out, but the disciples didn't really understand the mission His message was referring to - sending them out as His Father sent him to the earth. It was a challenging mission. If they had thought about it properly, they would have known that Jesus' sojourn on earth was difficult; embroiled with a lot of contingencies: the mission of possible imprisonment, torture or death, He was passing everything over to them.

During one of His last appearances to His disciples, Jesus continued to keep them strong and to make them prepared for the challenges ahead of them. He appeared to Peter and some other disciples who were fishing at the sea of Tiberia. They had fished all night without any success. At dawn, Jesus appeared at the shore and started to interact with them. There was no evidence that Jesus disguised Himself, but none of the disciples could recognize him. He told Peter and his peers to throw their net on the right side of their boat, and they caught unexpected huge quantity of fish. It was after this incident that one of the disciples suspected him and told Peter that it was the Lord. None of them confirmed it though it was the third time Jesus appeared to them since after his resurrection (John 21: 1 - 11).

He asked to have breakfast with them since it was normal for fishermen to eat breakfast at the shore. Jesus served them with fried fish and bread, and during this food serving, He was clearly revealed to them as their Lord. At this breakfast, Jesus asked Peter three times: "Do you love me?" (John 21: 12 -14).

He responded to the first question: "Yes, Lord, I love you." Jesus told him to Feed His Lamb; The second time, Peter answered: "Yes, Lord, you know I love you;" He told him to Feed His Sheep. The third question grieved Peter, possibly because of his past experience during the persecution where he denied Jesus three times before the cock crow (Luke 22: 61). Peter could not imagine why Jesus was asking him the same question for the third time. Three didn't seem to be a good number for Peter. However, he responded with humility: "Lord, you know my heart, you know that I love you;" Jesus said to him, "Feed my sheep" (John 21: 15 - 17).

"When you were young," Jesus said, "you were able to do as you liked and go wherever you wanted to; but when you are old, you will stretch out your hands and others will direct you and take you where you don't want to go" (John 21: 18). While He was trying to explain to Peter the type of death he would die to glorify God, He asked: "Follow me."

The disciples were over-whelmed with the joy of seeing their Master and Leader again. They began to reconnect to all that Jesus taught them earlier about his death and resurrection. However, this was a new beginning; like a disciple sent on apostolic work to China who, by knowing what he valued and wanted to achieve, he oriented himself and adapted confidently to the unfamiliar circumstances.[94]

The reality was evident in Paul's subsequent message to his brethens: "I think you ought to know, dear brothers, about the hard time we went through. ... We were really crushed and overwhelmed, and feared we would never live through it. We felt we were doomed to die and saw how powerless we were to help ourselves; but that was good, for then we put everything into the hands of God, who alone could save us, for he can even raise the dead. And he did help us, and saved us from a terrible death; yes, and we expect him to do it again and again." (2 Corinthians 1: 8 - 10)

Like St. John also wrote to his Christian brothers: "Again I say, we are telling you about what we ourselves have actually seen and heard, so that you may share the fellowship and the joys we have with the Father and with Jesus Christ his Son." (1 John 1: 3)

Pope John Paul II concluded one of his prayers saying: "Let us search for [God's] hand to guide us; and find in [him] the way, the truth, and the life."[95] It is true that things do not get better by being left alone. " A garden does not evolve into a better garden simply by allowing nature to take its course; the weeds will grow as well as the flowers."[96]

ALWAYS YOUR GOD

S eek for the Lord when He comes to your house, your church or when He passes through your way. Seek for Him when He is near. By all indications, He is ready to listen and come to your rescue. He promised never to fail you. When the sea is rough, and your ship is being tossed by the wave, call upon Him like Peter did: "Lord, save me!" (Matthew 14: 30 - 31) or I perish. Jesus stretched out his hand to the sinking Peter and saved him.

"It is hard to get direction if you don't know where you are."[97] There is no doubt that God is always stretching His hands to you but, are you watching? Are you stretching your own hand? A woman from Canaan cried to Jesus: Help me now, O Lord, thou son of David; my daughter is grievously vexed with a devil" Jesus did not disappoint her; He said to her: "O woman, great is thy faith: be it unto thee even as thou wilt." (Matthew 15: 22, 28). Another woman who had incurable blood disease, having her strong faith, took the privilege of getting close to Jesus and touched him while passing her way, she was made whole. Jesus told her to go in Peace (Mark. 5: 27 - 34).

Zacchaeus who was of a small stature wanted to reach-out to Jesus. He knew he wasn't much liked in the society because of his job as a tax collector, and would not be allowed if he asked of Jesus' followers. He struggled to reach-out to Jesus; he climbed up a sycomore tree, and when Jesus saw the great faith in Zacchaeus, He told him to come down; "I'm coming to your house today." (Luke 19: 5). Martha knew that her brother died but she had faith that Jesus could make the impossible to be possible. "...And even now it's not too late, for I know that God will bring my brother back to life again, if you will only ask Him to;" she told Jesus (John 11: 21). " I believe you are the Messiah, the Son of God, the one we have so long awaited." (John 11:27).

How was Martha rewarded for having such strong faith and conviction? Jesus told people to roll off the stones on the Lazarus tomb, and Jesus ordered him to come out. "And Lazarus came out in the grave-cloth, his face muffled in the bandage" and Jesus told the people there to unwrap Lazarus and let him go (John 11: 23 - 44).

While we have unlimited list of request for God and "occasionally daydream about arriving at pleasant destination in [*our*] efforts, it is important that you remember that movement is necessary for arrival."[98] It is important to know that one who truly lives under obedience is fully disposed to execute instantly and unhesitatingly whatever is enjoined him, no matter to him whether it be very hard to do.[99]

When the sea of your life roars and tumbles, and the swirling pinnacle seem to be unending, the manner and pattern in which you cope with it contributes to the outcome. Most of the time, you'll understand that realizing your desire involves having strong beliefs and nobility.

"It doesn't matter how close we are to the presence of Jesus;" said Archbishop Charles Chaput, "We can still completely ignore Him, and therefore never experience the transforming power of His Love."

The testimony of the poor blind man cannot be forgotten. The man used to beg at the street corners to make a living. His survival depended on the mercy of the people passing his way and showing some kindness. One day, he heard that Jesus was passing through his way. He was full of expectation because of what he had heard about Jesus. With all his faith and reverence, he started to look for a means to get some help from Him.

The blind man was at alert waiting to notice the passing of Jesus through him. It was an opportunity he did not want to miss. However, he had some big obstacles before him: one, where to position himself properly along the way so that Jesus could hear him when he called for help; two, how to overcome the large crowd around Jesus since He was known to attract multitude of followers.

Dr. Mahoney said that problem is an unpleasant feeling of discrepancy between the way things are and the way we would like them to be.[100] The blind man was determined to stay to the end but also worried about his chances of succeeding. But, he kept his faith and waited for his chance.

When the moment arrived and he perceived that Jesus was coming, coupled with the noises of people around Him, he began to shout out loud: "Jesus, son of David, have mercy on me!"

(Mark 10: 48). Some selfish people who wanted to frustrate his opportunity tried to drown his voice by screaming on him to stop shouting.

You must remember the number of times you have tried to pursue your dreams or to implement your life goals but your adversaries stood to frustrate your opportunity so that you would not get any help; they tried to detour your road so that you would not accomplish your desires at the proximate time.

What did the blind man do? Undaunted and unruffled by all the obstacles of the moment, he shouted louder and louder: "Jesus son of David, have mercy on me! Jesus son of David, have mercy on me!!"

When you attempt to find an effective solution to your problem, "what is important is that [your effort] be promising enough that it just might work - promising enough that you will be motivated to try it and give it a fair chance."[101] The fair chance worked because the poor blind beggar did not succumb, and Jesus heard his voice and responded.

Those who were trying to obstruct his endeavor to reach Jesus were marveled, and they started calling him a lucky man when Jesus stopped for him. "Tell him to come here," Jesus directed his disciples. The blind man was brought to Him. Nobody knew what Jesus was going to do for him but, it was obvious that the blind man's life would change for good (Mark 10:49- 50).

The news that Jesus the Son of God wanted to see him brought a big jubilation to the poor blind man. "What do you want me to do for you?" Jesus asked him. (Mark 10:51). Getting the attention of Jesus was the greatest blessing, and he knew it was a life time opportunity.

The blind man borrowing the Solomon's wisdom replied: "Lord, I want to see." He did not abuse the opportunity to ask for materials things. He asked for the most humble and relevant thing to him, "to see". "It is done! Your faith has healed you." (Mark 10: 52).

The experience of Solomon who at his youth was made a King, and he quickly realized that he lacked the knowledge to confront the responsibilities ahead of him in the midst of (God) chosen people, a nation so great and too many people to count! Solomon requested from God. "I am but a little child: I know not how to go out or come in" (I King 3: 5 - 7).

God knows our problems and the solutions to our problems but, most often, He leaves us with the responsibility of choices of preference, purpose and relevance. There are moments that we make bogus and overzealous demands from God. "When you plan consciously to succeed, you can choose both the quality and quantity of your productive effort."[102] If you are going the wrong direction, you can never get to your destination no matter how fast you go and how hard you try. You must take an exit to return to the right direction. Whatever choices and encounters you experience during this journey will have important values in your life.

Considering those who make inappropriate request, when two brothers, James and John had the opportunity to meet and ask for a favor from Jesus, He asked them: "what would you want me to do for you?" They replied that they would want to sit in his throne with him in his kingdom, one brother at his right hand and the other brother at his left. The response from Jesus was immediate and clear: "You don't know what you are asking for."

"It is not enough to be next to Jesus, or to approve of His teachings, or to know 'about' Him. We need to love Him. We need to be with Jesus, and in Jesus."[103]

"What shall I give you? God asked Solomon. With humility and selflessness, Solomon asked for wisdom: "Give your servant an understanding mind so that I can govern your people well and know the difference between what is right and what is wrong" (1 Kings 3: 9).

God was very happy with Solomon because he did not ask for riches, long life or vindication against his enemies but wisdom. "I will give you what you asked for" in abundance like no person before you had or after you would get. He also went further in giving him even the things he did not ask for: wealth and honor.

"God is not an unfeeling, cold-hearted monarch of heaven. He feels our pains; He shares our sorrows, He cares, and He considers each one of us important enough to love."[104] God sees our wounds, necessities and struggles, and cannot look away from people who look up to him for support.

When Peter and John were in distress, having been arrested and were about to be prosecuted for preaching and spreading the gospel of the Lord; they did not loose hope, but believed strongly in whom they were working for. They were strong in spirit and mind, knowing that they would not be forgotten. When they did not expect to be rescued, God sent his angel by night to open the prison door and let them free. (Acts.5:19).

When Daniel defied all odds and trusted in the Lord, he was delivered. He told King Darius who ordered him to be thrown unto the den of lions: "My God hath sent his angel, and hath shut the lions' mouth, that they have not hurt me ..." (Daniel 6: 22)   When Goliath said that he would kill David and give his flesh to birds and wild animals, and David replied that he would conquer Goliath and prove to the world that the battle was the Lord's battle that didn't need sword and spear. (1 Samuel 17: 46 - 50). He did it and the world glorified God.

This is the God of eternity: the God of yesterday, today and forever. He will fight your war, rescue you from all iniquity and adversaries. "Humble yourself therefore under the mighty hand of God, that he may exalt you in due time" (1 Peter. 5: 6). "When our mind is intent on temporal things in order that it may rest in them, it remains immersed therein; but when it is intent on them in relation to the acquisition of beatitude, it is not lowered by them, but raises them to a higher level."[105]

"Nothing ought to be more binding on us than the business of heaven ... ." "To this we ought to apply ourselves with all our endeavors, and not to be slack, however necessary or urgent are the things that draw us aside"[106] It is true that human life transient, and Augustine went further to say: "All that we touch passes away, and well it should; for all that we touch is good if it leads us home to God, but bad if it keeps us from him."[107] Unless you are energetic in tempo, manner, faith, and make the connection with God, otherwise your efforts may be punctuated.

Our relationship with God, and our journey to the paradise of God cannot be with anxiety nor can we wish our way to it. It is not a journey of days or months but unregulated timing, and going to an immeasurable distance. If you jump into this journey unprepared and with a wild ambition, you will fail and your faith will decline and die.

Archbishop Charles Chaput told us to examine the genuineness of our feelings toward God without dwelling in pre-maturity. "[W]e should also remember that in this world, feelings can be fickle. They're hot and cold; they come and go. Ultimately, it's not how we 'feel' that shapes how genuine our encounter with Jesus is."[108]

Some of the times, you run to God because you are frustrated, desperate, and disillusioned with what you need at the moment. Human beings are sneaky and disobedient, they run away and forget God soon after their problems are solved. Some people don't worship God because of the love of worshiping but are afraid of the consequences of not worshiping. Humans change with their social status, they don't worry about God when they don't need him. They call on God because they need him.

When the partying is over and reality sets in, they start looking for God. There is the saying that human beings are "selfish creatures who struggle for resources, pleasure, and prestige, and [they] were shaped by group selections to be hive creatures who long to lose [them]selves in something larger."[109] The Israelites went against Moses who saved them from the hands of Pharaoh. The merriment was over and things became rough, they accused Moses of taking them out from the land of Egypt into the desert claiming it was flowing with milk and honey for selfish reasons. These were the same people who had praised God for their victory saying: "You have led the people you redeemed. But in your loving kindness You have guided them wonderfully to your holy land" (Exodus 15: 13).

Moses was humiliated by the Israelites, some of them told him that he was only motivated by the desire to make himself a Prince over them than showing a real care. (Numb. 16: 13). They had forgotten how they were kept in bondage in the land of Egypt. All the things Moses had done for them became things of the past. They forgot when Pharaoh made their lives bitter with hard bondage, in morter, and in brick, and in all manners of services, wherein they were given hard labor. (Exodus 1: 14). They did not appreciate any more the crossing of the red sea, at the time of hunger and thirsty, being provided with manna and water from the rock at the desert.

And God said that the Israelites were stiff-necked. You could imagine how Moses felt about his people's: rejection, ingratitude, insatiability and unfaithfulness. Interestingly, despite all their disobedience and anger, Moses did not give-up on his people. He continued to plead to God on their behalf.

"Call upon me in the day of trouble: I will deliver thee and you shall glorify me." (Psalm 50:15). That's all God asks for, to be glorified. The glorification of God is a mere expression of our appreciation of what he has been doing for us. "We are creatures who are not our own beginning, not the masters of adversity, not our own last end."[110]

The ingratitude did not stop with the Israelites; when Jesus cured the ten lepers, only one came back to glorify Him. "Didn't I heal ten men? Where are the nine?" Jesus asked. (John 17:17-18). When we feel fulfilled and satisfied with ourselves and when we are carried away with the sugars and honeys of the world, we forget or hesitate to thank God for providing those things for us.

God gives us gifts on two prominent conditions : 1) the ones He provides to us whether we ask for them or not because He knows we need them - He provides for us even when we don't deserve those things. 2) "He gives us on condition we put ourselves in the area of His Love."[111]

A battle field is never stagnant, it's always shifting and the soldiers change as circumstances warrant. A soldier does not quit from fighting because the battle field changed; that is the true life. Quitters never win. The only one who is consistent at all times and at all places is God, and will always be with you when you fight his battle.

There was a man, Chuck, whose dad died before his first birthday, and his mom followed five years later. He was raised by his elder sister who struggled hard to put food on the table. Saying that they lived below poverty level was an understatement. Every day was a war of survival, surprisingly you wouldn't notice it on him. He was religious, always attending church activities and was self-confident. You may think he would be begging around for help; No. He was very appreciative when people did him a favor but, rarely did he complain of anything. He would stay the whole day without any food and no one outside his house would know about it.

At the age of 16, his sister who had been there for him died. It was like a bolt from the blue for him. There was no money for his sister's funeral until a benefactor intervened and paid all the bills. And thereafter, it was difficult to know how to move on. Although he had a big heart and wanted to stay in their small house which he had shared with his sister all his life, but it was obvious he would encounter some stormy weathers. He refused being adopted by people who wanted to help. He was determined to fight for his own survival.

He continued being humble and attending church every Sunday. You would think he would be angry with God for his miserable life and for God not intervening in his causes. No. None of those things happened but he continued to grow in strength and wisdom; appreciating people who helped him. There were moments you would think he had been torn trying to control the barriers of life, but he would show such resistance that defied description. He overcame all his difficulties and, went as far as completing his high school education with wonderful results.

With a help from a good Samaritan, he left his small town to a big city. He quickly got a job. It was a minimum wage job but it was a better income than he had ever earned in his life. He worked hard and the job offered him an opportunity to attend a part time college courses at one of the Universities. He was proud of himself as his job status continued to improve and his education was getting better.

He maintained his job until he graduated. Without any doubt, the University degree pushed him up the ladder in the company. He was able to get an apartment of his own before getting married few months later. He started feeling like his life was changing for good.

As if God was asleep for him and did not wish his sore wound to heal, his wife had difficulty conceiving for a baby. This was a man who loved children and wanted to have one of his own. All the doctors' visits, marriage counseling, praying and fasting seemed to be wasted efforts.

After about ten years of marriage, trying and without any success to get any child, he and his wife accepted their condition to be permanent. They decided to adopt a new baby girl, and the little girl became a source of joy to them. A little over one year of the adoption, he lost his job where he had almost reached to the top of administrative leadership level. The company went bankrupt and he lost all his benefits and privileges. It was like a Job's rerun. He still remembered the saying of St. James: "Blessed is the man that endureth temptation: for when he is tried, he shall receive the crown of life, which the Lord hath promised to them that love him." (James 1:12).

The most amazing thing was that he did not lose his faith. "Faith" as St. Thomas Aquinas described, "is necessary to God to whom we pray; that is, we need to believe that we can obtain from Him what we seek.[112] He also added that patience is chiefly needed to enable us to preserve, and to bear all the troubles which come upon us in this world."[113]

The family was surviving on his wife's average income until he got another small job to supplement his wife's. After about another year, his wife conceived. It didn't seem to be real even when their family doctor confirmed it. Again, they didn't want to celebrate it but continued to watch. They lived their normal lives, avoided being over excited.

The scripture said: "God is our refuge and strength, a very present help in trouble"; (Psalm. 46: 1) when it was time, it was a baby boy and they called him Emmanuel - God is with us. This family which thought they found themselves in a world of unconquerable hope, now dwell in joy that has no boundary. Since that time, the future of the family has been on the positive side.

"The Lord is good; his mercy is everlasting; and his truth endureth to all generations." (Psalm 100: 5). And, Thomas Aquinas strenghtens us when fighting the turmoil that come to our lives: "This gift of fortitude prevents man's heart from fainting through fear of lacking necessities, and makes him trust without wavering that God will provide him whatever he needs..."[114]

Record has shown that no one who stood firmed and strong, and walking by the way of wisdom has regretted it. "It belongs to perseverance to persevere to the end of the virtuous work, for instance that a soldier persevere to the end of the fight, and the magnificent man until his work be accomplished...."[115] The Lord hears the righteous cry and delivers him out of all his troubles (Psalm 34:17).

St Paul wrote to the Ephesians: "Put on the whole armor of God, that you may be able to stand against the wiles of the devil. For we wrestle not against flesh and blood, but against principalities, against powers, against the rulers of the darkness of this world, against spiritual wickedness in high places. Stand therefore, having your lions girt about with truth, and having on the breastplate of righteousness; ... Above all, taking the shield of faith, wherewith you shall be able to quench all the fiery darts of the wicked. And take helmet of salvation, the sword of the Spirit, which is the word of God: Praying always with all prayer and supplication in the Spirit, and watching thereunto with all perseverance and supplication for all saints" (Ephesians 6: 11 - 18).

This world is a highway; when you are driving on this highway, you cannot slumber. While being sober and vigilant, the scripture asked you never to be weary or stumble; you should belt and bootstraps because your adversary the devil is a roaring lion. To save yourself, you should escape as the deer escape from the hunters and bird from the net. The fascinating point, the scripture asked you to be wise and learn from the ants (Proverb: 5 - 6).

It was in the same spirit that Paul wrote: "Therefore, my beloved brethren, be you steadfast, always abounding in the work of the Lord, forasmuch as you know that your labor is not in vain in the Lord" (1 Corinthians 15: 58). It was this steadfastness that Job reiterated, when he said it would take away your fear and make you to forget your misery like a passed away water (Job 11: 15 -16).

BIBLIOGRAPHY

1) Restoration of Reason, Montague Brown, ed. 2006 (United States of America), 159

2) For the Love of Wisdom, Josef Pieper, (2006 Ignatius Press, San Franscisco) 306

3) Catechism of the Catholic Church, Pope John Paul II, (First Image, April, 1995, New York) 21

4) Restoration of Reason, 161

5) Guide to Thomas Aquinas, Josef Pieper, (Ignatius, San Francisco) 137

6) Augustine, James J. O'Dennell, 74

7) Restoration of Reason, 114-115

8) The Philosophy of Tolkien, Peter J. Kreeft, (2005, Ignatius, San Francisco), 49

9) Augustine, 68

10) Williams James, Writings 1901 - 1910, 291

11) Ibid, 253

12) Letter to My Brother Priests, Pope John Paul II, 147

13) Catechism, 694/5

14) Williams James, 416

15) Ibid

16) World Hunger, Gerald J. A. Nwankwo, 114

17) Life is Worth Living, Fulton J. Sheen, (1999 Ignatius, San Francisco), 271

18) Beating the Odds, Rev. Msgr Anselm Nwaorgu, 7

19) Williams James, 461

20) Beating the Odds, 9

21) Reflection on a Dying Life, Donald X. Burt, 95

22) Augustine, 103

23) Ibid, 113

24) Ibid, 114

25) Williams James, 177/8

26) Letter to My Brother Priests, 19

27) The Private Prayers of Pope John Paul II - An Invitation to Prayer, 28

28) The Word Among Us, Lent 2013, 84

29) St. Thomas Aquinas - A Treasury of Quotations On The Spiritual life, 219

30) Give Us This Day, 7 October 2012

31) Sermon in a Sentence - St Thamos Aquinas, John P. McClernon, 225

32) The Unthinkable Touch of Grace, Cherryl Richardson, 206

33) The Private Prayers of Pope John Paul - A Life in Prayer, 75

34) I am Second, Dough Bender, Dave Sterret, 28

35) Williams James, 260

36) United States Catholic Catechism for Adults, 39

37) The Reason for God, Timothy Keller, 173

38) Animal Farm, George Orwell, 11

39) The Trial and Death of Socrates (Four Dialogues), Plato, 65

40) Catechism of The Catholic Church, 274

41) Ibid, 276

42) Ibid, 275

43) Seeds of Contemplation, Thomas Merton, 36

44) Reflection on a Dying Life, 103

45) Catechism, 692

46) The Reason for God, Timothy Keller, 162

47) Prayer and Devotions, Pope John Paul II, 89

48) The Happiness Hypothesis, Jonathan Haidt, 84

49) Anonymous

50) The Unmistakable Touch of Grace, 54

51) John Paul II and the Meaning of Suffering, Robert G. Schroeder

52) Reflection on a Dying Life, 21

53) Seeds of Contemplation, 47

54) Beating the Odds, 75

55) Hold on to your faith - When God Doesn't Make Sense, Dr. James Dobson, 38

56) John Paul II and the Meaning of Suffering, Robert G. Schroeder, 63

57) Sermon in a Sentence - Vol. 5, St. Thomas Aquinas, John P. McClernon, 108

58) Beating the Odds, 56

59) The Reason For God, Timothy Keller, 166

60) Williams James, 47

61) Sermon in a Sentence, 99

62) Williams James, 277

63) Augustine, 21

64) John Paul II and the Meaning of Suffering, 131

65) The Philosophy of Tolkien, 150

66) Reflections On a Dying Life, 64

67) Life Is Worth Living, 267

68) Ibid

69) Augustine, 18

70) World Hunger, Gerald J.A. Nwankwo, 141

71) The Trial and Death of Socrates, 83

72) Love of Wisdom, 59

73) ABC News 11/14/12

74) The Trial of Socrates, I.F. Stone, 69

75) Crossing The Threshold of Hope, Pope John Paul II, 188

76) The Psychology of Self Esteem, Nathaniel Brandem, 117

77) Reflection On a Dying Life, 63

78) Augustine, 22

79) Beating the Odds, 72

80) Williams James, 289

81) Augustine, 61

82) Letters to My Brother Priests, 15

83) Heroic Leadership, Chris Lowney, 24

84) The Trial and Death of Socrates, 44

85) Life is Worth Living, 270

86) Ibid, 272

87) An Invitation to Prayer, Pope John Paul II, 20

88) Strength in Darkness - John of the Cross, 62

89) I am Second

90) Ibid

91) Reflection on the Dying, 129

92) I am Second, Doug Bender, Dave Sterret, 177

93) Ibid

94) Heroic Leadership, 20

95) An Invitation to Prayer, 89

96) Life Is Worth Living, 98

97) Self Change: Strategies for Solving Personal Problems, Micheal J. Mahoney, 55

98) Ibid 114

99) Heroic Leadership,49

100) Self Change, 25

101) Ibid,106

102) Beating the Odds

103) The Catholic Standard & Times, (May 12, 2012), 5

104) You Are Extraordinary - Tract - Good News Publisher

105) Sermon in a Sentence, 56

106) Ibid, 98

107) Augustine, 22

108) The Catholic Standard & Times, (May 2012), 5

109) The Happiness Hypothesis, Jonathan Haidt, 238

110) Catechism, 694

111) Life is Worth Living, 273

112) Sermon in a Sentence, 226

113) Ibid, 104

114) Ibid, 103

115) Ibid, 101